THIS TWISTED PATH

This Twisted Path

My Journey Through Abuse and Addiction in Amish Country

MONROE MILLER

LIONCREST
PUBLISHING

THIS TWISTED PATH

My Journey through Abuse and Addiction in Amish Country

ISBN   978-1-5445-1829-9   *Hardcover*
       978-1-5445-1828-2   *Paperback*
       978-1-5445-1827-5   *Ebook*

I WOULD LIKE TO DEDICATE THIS BOOK
TO MY LOVELY WIFE, ESTHER.

Contents

Introduction

To this day, I can still get triggered by hairy arms.

I was a very young boy growing up in the Amish community when I was sexually molested by an older man. I remember the pain and trying to bite. From that moment on, in my mind, everybody was out to hurt me. My first defense was to bite. My counselors have told me I've blocked almost everything else out from that period of time, but I am still triggered. Sometimes I will panic. Sometimes I can still remember the taste, the smell. It's been so long ago, but it's never left me.

Even though I blocked most of it out, I know it controlled how I thought and how I reacted to people and places over the years, though I wasn't even aware of it at the time. For a long time, I didn't trust men. You will notice in this book that the people I trusted or have been close to are almost all women.

Because of my abuse, I built walls around myself that became almost impenetrable. I couldn't feel the love and companionship that others could. This, in turn, made me feel like an outcast. Alone. It is just a vicious circle. As I grew, I turned to drugs to block it all out. It was my only way of dealing with the pain. My recovery truly started when I was in drug rehab and I realized that I wasn't the only one that this happened to. I honestly don't know of anyone that I went to rehab with who hadn't been sexually molested. That's a horrible, sad truth. So, if you're reading this and you understand even a little of what I'm writing about…know you are not alone. I promise.

This book is not all about sexual molestation. It is about my path, however twisted. I am writing it to tell you my story. And yes, my story *does* start with the abuse. I won't go into too much detail, but it was where it all began. But there's more in this book—my story of growing up in the Amish community, of marrying the love of my life, of becoming addicted to opioids, of rehab. It's also a story of community, of moving through trauma, and of faith.

To tell you the truth, deciding whether or not to write this book was the hardest decision I have ever made. To tell the whole world your secrets and your fears? To share with them your hopes and dreams? To know that everyone you meet will look at you differently? It's scary. My wife and I had long discussions about whether to move forward. We prayed about it for a long time. We decided that the simple fact that I'm alive to tell my story, while there are thousands of cemeteries around the world where mothers grieve at headstones of children who were taken from them by the beast that is addiction, is reason enough.

Looking back, I can see I was afraid of facing my fears, of facing what was hurting me. I felt getting help was admitting there was something wrong with me, but the first step to recovery is to admit that something is wrong. It's been a long road, but I am at peace now. It's sad that I lived with that all those years, but at long last I'm free. Truly free. It's so exhilarating, sometimes I just look to the sky and smile. The world around me seems brighter and more colorful. All my problems seem smaller and easier to deal with. I imagine that's how a butterfly feels in the spring.

To think of all the lonely, hurting children out there still is just heartbreaking to me. This world can be such a dark, lonely place without someone you can trust with your terrible secret. My beautiful, patient wife gets all the credit for starting me on the road to recovery. She was the one to first recognize the signs and really push me to get help. She is such an unbelievably strong person.

Together, we agreed that if I could help even *one* person by writing this book, it would all be worth it.

Maybe that one person will be you, or someone you know. Even if not, my hope is that from my story, we can treat each other with a little more grace. We never know what other people have been through or are going through.

Thank you for reading.

CHAPTER ONE

My Path Begins

Growing Up Amish

T started on my path February 17, 1986 as the first-born child of a young Amish couple, Marvin and Anna Miller, who grew up near Kidron, Ohio. My mom had four brothers and ten sisters, and my dad had two sisters. As of this writing, I have ninety-eight first cousins. This is one example of how, in our community, there is always plenty of love to go around.

In the Amish lifestyle, everything is done manually. We have horses and buggies instead of cars. The men wear pants, suspenders, and hats, and the women wear dresses, capes, and bonnets. We don't have electricity, technology, or television—but we always have each other. Everything the Amish do is family-oriented, in fact, and I consider myself privileged to have grown up in this environment. Though we grew up very poor, I had loving parents, brothers and sisters, a warm bed, and that was enough for me. My world was a small one, but I was content.

As a kid, I knew that we lived a different lifestyle than most of the world, but I never gave it much thought. We played, fought, loved, and prayed together. We made our own magic and mischief. I have a million small memories to prove it—like in the winter, when Mom would bring the clothes off the line, they'd be frozen stiff as boards. Sometimes we'd chase each other around the house, trying to smack each other with them. At home we spoke Pennsylvania Dutch, and when I heard the English language, it seemed so exotic.

I never questioned how we lived or thought that I may be missing out. In my later years, I was called many derogatory names (like "backwards") by people who just can't see past the clothes we wear or how we do everything by hand—but in my childhood, I knew nothing else.

Because we didn't have technology, we used our imaginations to keep us entertained. That's one reason toys are extremely important to Amish kids. A little Amish girl's most prized possession, for example, is almost always her doll. As young boys, our favorite toys were anything we could make noise with. One toy stood out to me, though: nothing topped the miniature farm. We could spend hours playing with the tiny tractors, making sure we got the harvest in before the winter hit, keeping the animals in the pasture, and taking the young livestock to auctions. Of course, even the best-kept farms could be destroyed in seconds by a young sibling blundering onto your property, knocking down fences and stealing animals and machinery.

Our imaginations came in handy outside the house too. If we saw something exciting in the outside world, we would re-create it in our minds and put our own spin on it. Once, after seeing an air show, my brothers and cousins and I made tiny parachutes out of handkerchiefs and attached them to sticks. We threw them out of the upstairs windows. Some would drift down perfectly, but the unlucky sticks would plummet straight to their deaths.

Growing up as Amish kids also meant we were always sur-rounded by animals, and at an early age we were taught the responsibility of taking care of them. Sometimes we would get distracted by our daily adventures, but when Dad came home from work at the lumber mill, we knew we had better get the chores done in a hurry.

In my family, we also had our own personal rabbits we had to nurture and take care of. We took great pride in growing and grooming them to maturity. We spent countless hours taking them out of their cages and playing with them in the yard, pretending they were our kids. My sisters liked to give theirs rides in doll strollers, but my rabbit was much more manly. He would get rides on the back of my dump truck—that is, until my brother killed him with a brick.

During my childhood, I had many animals I will never forget: one was my dog Jake, a huge German shepherd that scared everybody but me and my family. He would not let anybody near us unless Mom or Dad told him it was OK. If I had to go do the chores outside after dark, for example, I would go to the door and whistle until he showed up. He would always stay by my side until I was done. One summer night, I was in the barn doing chores when I heard a car pull into the driveway. Instantly, I felt Jake tense up and heard him growl. I turned off my light and, with him by my side, snuck around the barn and up along the house. As the man got out of the car and started up the sidewalk, I could tell he was a stranger. Just as he was ready to knock, I flashed my light on him. At the same time, Jake let loose, viciously snarling and barking. Who was it? It turns out the poor victim standing in my light was just an old man who was just dropping off some oranges for us. He later told Dad it was one of the most terrifying experiences of his life. Dad later asked me if I hadn't been afraid—but to be honest, it hadn't even crossed my mind. That's just how much I trusted Jake to take care of me.

When we lost Jake, it was devastating. One evening when I was outside playing, I heard Dad call for Jake. He was slowly crossing the road in a crouch because he knew he wasn't supposed to be across the road. I saw the car come flying over the hill, and I felt a sinking in my gut. Jake was hit in midair, the impact tossing him across the gravel driveway. I reached Jake about the same time Dad did, and we could tell from one look that my companion had no chance. He lifted his head and whined a little, but from his rib cage to his tail was a mangled mess. Dad turned and immediately headed for the house. I knew he was heading to get the shotgun, so I followed him to try and talk him out of it. In my child's mind, I thought maybe we could still fix Jake somehow. Dad quietly told me he had to do it because Jake was in terrible pain, and we couldn't just let him suffer like that. When it happened, I held my hands over my ears as hard as I could, but I still heard the shot. I can still hear it to this day, to tell you the truth.

WHEN IT ALL STARTED: ABUSE

I don't know how old I am, but I know I am barely walking. I don't know where I am, but I know I am outside. I remember trying to bite his arm and getting slapped in the face. I remember the taste. Thinking I was going to choke. Not being able to breathe. The hair on his arms, his other hair in my face. I remember seeing my pacifier laying in the dirt in front of me. I want to get to it so badly.

CHURCH CHALLENGES

One pillar of the Amish lifestyle is family, and the other is faith. We had church every other Sunday, and with very few exceptions, we all had to go. (If you're wondering why it's every other Sunday, it's to give ministers from other congregations a chance to visit each other's churches. This also gives the congregation a chance to hear different ministers on any given Sunday.)

When it was time for church, Mom and Dad would get up early. Dad would go get the horse ready, and Mom would wake my siblings and I up, feed us breakfast, and help us put on our Sunday clothes. After both my parents were ready and in their own church clothes, we'd do a morning prayer and be on our way. Even though church is core to the Amish identity, that didn't come easy for me—especially as a young boy. In fact, I absolutely hated going to church. I didn't admit it to anyone for years, but it was likely obvious by how I acted.

In an Amish church, the men and women sit separately. Because of the sexual abuse I'd suffered at the hands of an older man, I could not stand having to sit with the men in church. I would start getting nervous the Saturday evening before, and by the time we would arrive at church, my stomach would be in a hard knot. I could only take sitting in that situation for so long before I would start to feel like the walls were closing in. It would become harder to breathe, and I couldn't focus on anything except getting out and away from everybody.

In my panic, desperate to get away from the men, I acted

out in every way possible: screaming, throwing things, and hitting other kids. I'm pretty sure that I hold the record for most spankings in church by an Amish kid. I didn't like the spankings, of course, but I remember thinking they were worth it because at least they got me out for a few moments.

In the summertime, church services were sometimes held in someone's barn instead of in a home. Usually that didn't bother me because there was more space, though I certainly still had my moments where I simply could not take it anymore. My poor parents were at their wit's end dealing with me. As I got older and became more able to use my words, they would question me about why I hated going to church. But I couldn't tell them it was because it reminded me of the abuse. And I never did.

As I got older, my punishments changed: instead of getting spanked, Dad would give me more work to do at home—something I hated a lot more than the spanking. The way I looked at it, a spanking didn't last long, but work could last all day.

Not every weekend was awful for me. Those in-between Sundays when we did not have church were another story altogether. I loved those days—the whole family together at home, having meals, listening to Bible stories, playing tag or hide-and-seek, coming around the table to play board games and snack on Kool-Aid and popcorn. Those days were wonderful and such a stark contrast to how I felt on church Sundays.

As I look back on my behavior during those years, I give my parents a lot of credit for the patience they showed their little troublemaker. In their own ways, they tried to help me overcome what ailed me about church. Mom would try to get me excited about playing with the other boys my age after church, for example, but it never worked. Because of what had happened to me, my self-confidence was not there like it was for other boys. I felt different, like everyone was better than me. In my heart, I just knew they wouldn't want to play with me. I knew I could never be on the same level they were. My peers interpreted my anxiety and low self-esteem as aloofness, and I got picked on a lot. If they were mean or spiteful to me, it only served to reinforce what I already knew in my young mind: I didn't deserve their friendship or love. I wasn't worth it.

To survive, I learned at an early age to hate myself and to never show emotion. Instead, I would bottle up all my feelings until I would explode in a temper tantrum. These outbursts only further served to alienate me from the other kids. Every night, I went to bed thinking how I was so different from them and wondering what I would be faced with next.

FAMILY TIES

Though I was miserable in church and around other kids my age, I felt genuinely happy around my family.

My very first memory, in fact, is from when I was very young: Dad's friend had raised deer, and he'd taken me to visit the farm to look at them. Later that night, Dad was swinging me on the porch swing, and I fell asleep. When I opened my eyes, I saw a deer staring right at me from the edge of the porch. I began to cry. Dad asked if I wanted my mom, and I nodded my head. When he took me to her and I saw her, I felt totally safe and loved. This memory is exceptionally clear to me, although I was very little. The night was warm and soft, and the sun had just gone down. What I remember most was the light on Mom's face and how she smiled when she saw me. It's one of the few times in my life that I have ever felt that sense of security.

I felt that kind of warmth from my family more as I got older, and one place I felt it often was at my grandma and grandpa's. Grandma was always waiting with a smile when my siblings and I would arrive. My aunts, especially Ruth, Miriam, and Bertha, would be waiting too—but to tease us unmercifully. They couldn't wait to hug, squeeze, and kiss us. I never minded the hugs or squeezes, but there was certainly a time I thought I was too big to be kissed. It hurt my manly pride, which was probably why they did it.

Grandma always had a candy jar on the counter just waiting for us to sneak into, and there were fresh baked goods too. If we needed a scrape soothed or a fight broken up, she was there. She was always fair and kind, and one of my favorite things about her was that, in my mind, she treated me like a grownup. She had this way of making me feel I was the only one in the world who mattered. The earliest memory I have of her is when my brother Wes was born. Mom and Dad were at the hospital, and Grandpa and Grandma were babysitting me and my sister Mattie. I was fine until it was time for bed, but then I broke down and started crying for my mom. Grandma started rocking me and singing "Will the Circle Be Unbroken." I will never forget that night, sitting in her lap, hearing her heartbeat in one ear and her singing in the other. It was one other time I felt totally safe and protected.

SPECIAL MEMORIES

Every once in a while, after much pleading and begging, I got to stay at my grandparents' overnight *alone* (and not when one of my siblings were being born—just because). Those were some of the highlights of my life—to be by myself at Grandpa's, knowing that the next day I would have the scooters all to myself, able to ride to my heart's content.

On those evenings, we would sit on the front porch swing until it got dark. Grandma would go inside and light the gas lamp, and Grandpa would follow, calling me after him. He would always sit at the head of the table, read the newspaper, and sip his final cup of coffee while Grandma fussed about the kitchen. Sometimes, before bedtime prayers, I could convince my aunts to help me catch fireflies. It was so fun to run around in the dark trying to catch them—and sometimes each other. When we were worn out, we'd sit on the porch and watch our fireflies blinking away. If I close my eyes, I can still hear the hiss of that gas lamp Grandma lit, remember the rustle of those pages Grandpa turned, and smell my cousins' freshly washed hair as we admired our blinking fireflies.

The very best times were when I got to stay over on a Friday night. That meant that the next day, Grandpa would be going to Kidron, and he would always take me along if I was there. Kidron was a small town, but it had sale barns, a flea market, a grocery store, and a hardware store. Together, they turned it into a bustling, vibrant place on Saturdays. The old men on benches would talk about the weather, the crop prices, and whatever old men talk about. The younger men would walk the flea markets, the young women would shop for groceries, and the kids would meet up and tell tall tales.

I was always so excited to go along that I could hardly wait until he had the horse hitched up. It would seem like forever before he was finally ready to go. We always took his rattling old wagon and his slow old horse. I didn't mind the slow pace, though, because it gave me more time to ask Grandpa more questions. Sometimes, he would hand me the reins and ask me to drive for a while. In those moments, I was on top of the world!

When we got to Kidron, I would wait while he took care of the horse. Then, I'd follow him toward the sale barn. I loved everything about the sale barns—the spittoons, the buckets of peanuts passed around, the noise and smell of the animals, the fast talking of the auctioneer. After the sale, he would take me across the boardwalk above the animals so I could see them in their pens. Eventually, we'd make our way back out to the flea market where the vendors would have their tables set up with everything you could imagine. Then, we'd get ice cream cones and eat them on one of the benches where Grandpa would soon be surrounded by friends and people who knew him. As a little boy, I remember thinking in those moments that my grandpa must have known all the people in the world.

On the way home, Grandpa would always have a buggy whip in his hand. Though I never saw him use it on his horse, he would use it on everything else, absentmindedly tapping any-thing and everything within range of his whip. I'm confident there is not one mailbox post, bush, or tree close to the road within a four-mile radius of his house that hasn't felt his whip.

One evening after supper, Wes came running into the house very excited.

"Grandma and Grandpa are coming! Grandma and Grandpa are coming," he yelled.

Mom, who was at the sink doing the dishes, turned around, wiping her hands on her apron.

"Are you sure?" she asked.

"Yes, I saw him whip a mailbox!" Wes said.

SHENANIGANS

Another benefit of going to my grandparents' house was the fact that Mom's brother, Ammon, lived at the end of the driveway, and they had three boys at the time. Daniel and Myron were a little older than me, but Bennie and I were close to the same age. We have been almost inseparable ever since I can remember. Even back then, if one of us got in trouble, the other one did too. We both had wild imaginations, and when we got together, we put them to good use.

Many of the more memorable shenanigans happened when one of my aunts or uncles were going through rumspringa. Rumspringa is a period of self-discovery for most Amish teenagers, usually starting at age sixteen or seventeen and continuing until anywhere from age nineteen to twenty-five. During rumspringa, you start making new friends, meeting new people, and experimenting with parts of the outside world like technology, music, and alcohol. It's also when you begin dating. This is a time of immense change for teens— one where you can explore your options and decide whether you want to join the church and help it grow or whether you want to take your own path. If you decide to join the church and get baptized, you become a member for life.

Joining the church is not a small act in the Amish community. They don't want anybody who isn't committed to living their life in Christ and helping the church in any way possible. Instead, they want someone willing to help pay hospital bills of fellow church members, assist widowers and widows, and aid the elderly. The bill piece is important to understand. We believe in helping each other in times of need instead of taking the traditional Western route, which would entail having insurance. Instead, if anybody in the church community were to have a flood or a house or barn fire, for example, everybody in the church would chip in to help rebuild it. If a church member were to have a medical cost he or she could not cover, the community would hold a benefit auction to help.

Rumspringa is a significant point of transition: either you choose to leave the Amish, or you stay and become part of the church. Most stay; there is a strong sense of security in knowing that if something should happen to you, that your family is taken care of for life.

Because of the freedom that comes with rumspringa, though,

my aunts' and uncles' bedrooms were treasure troves to us. We'd rummage through their closets looking for "English" clothes to try on. They always hid their stereos, but if we were lucky, we'd find a cassette tape somewhere. If we did, we'd quickly take it out on the upstairs porch and throw it down to one of our partners in crime, who would take off running for the woods. When we'd reconvene, safely hidden in the trees, we'd break open the tape and see how long we could stretch the spool of string inside.

Every once in a while, some of our aunts and uncles would have friends over for the weekend, and they would go back in the woods to have a bonfire and drink alcohol. Afterward, my cousins and I would go back, searching for any leftover beers. It rarely happened, but every once in a while, we would find one. We would all gather around eagerly, awaiting our turn for a sip of the warm, nasty stuff. We didn't show that it was nasty, though. Instead, we'd all pretend it was the greatest thing we'd ever tasted, but I think secretly we all knew the truth. That's probably why everyone would take only one sip, agreeing to dump it out afterward so nobody "got drunk." Sometimes, when searching these campsites, we'd find a lighter and try to smoke any cigarette butts we could find.

I didn't always get along with my cousins, though. We fought, as you do when you grow. One key argument that sticks out in my mind starts when my parents gave me a wooden pistol for Christmas—a big deal, because money was tight. It had a cocking hammer that came down when you pulled the trigger. I loved that pistol so much that I even took it to bed with me. It was always at my side, and I shot everything my imagination could conjure up. I had endless "hunting" adventures. Then came the day Mom invited her sisters for a party. There were a lot of kids there, and I wanted to hide my pistol. Mom pushed back, however, giving me the old lecture about sharing with others.

A couple of boys played with it, but after a while, they didn't have it anymore. When I questioned them about it, they said they'd hidden it. I didn't believe that they would be so cruel. I kept pestering them, but they wouldn't budge.

After they went home, I was desperate. Mom and I looked everywhere, but we had no luck. In the months to come, every time I saw one of those boys, I'd ask what they'd done with my gun. At first they'd say they took it home. Later, they'd say they didn't remember—which, to be fair, was probably true. A year or so later we moved to different place, and I knew deep down in my heart that I'd never see my gun again. I was devastated.

Years later, the man who moved into our old home asked Dad if I could come work for him during the summer. It wasn't long after I started working for him that I asked if he had ever, by chance, found a toy gun somewhere on his property. I described it for him and told him the story. When—to my shock—he brought it out and handed it to me, I had to fight back tears. Though it had been years, holding the toy gun brought back so many precious memories. It looked and felt just like I'd remembered it, and it still does. I keep that little gun in my gun safe, even today. Every once in a while, I take it out and sit with the memories of an innocence long lost.

CHAPTER TWO

A Rocky Start

Coming of Age

For me, kindergarten was held in a one-room schoolhouse called Maple Grove. During that time, my family and I still lived about half a mile away, so we walked there and back. But we weren't alone. Our neighbors—specifically Steven and Juanita—would walk with us. Steven was a ball of fire, quick and always smiling. His life came to a tragic end when he was twenty-three when he was killed in a corn field. He was throwing tomatoes at passing cars and buggies, and a man shot him. When I heard about this much later, the first thing that went through my mind was how Steven used to walk in front of me to school, offering to break the wind.

On those walks, his older sister, Juanita, had a special knack for knowing when I needed help, and she was very motherly to me. It was after she graduated that things started to go downhill for me. Without her to stand up for me, I got picked on.

BULLYING

My mistreatment in school started early, and I'm sure most of it stemmed from the fact that I had already unconsciously alienated myself from other kids. It was hard for me to play games with others, for example, because in my mind I was different. I was always trying to hide that fact from them, which only served to deepen the gap between us and make me look like a target.

Several memories come to mind: once, one of the older boys tied me to a post in the basement and taunted me, making fun of me and my family. The thought of those hairy arms started running through my head, and I started to panic. As I struggled to get out of the ties that were binding me both physically and mentally, the rope rubbed my wrists raw. The more I struggled, the funnier it was to them. But I didn't care. I just wanted to get away and go someplace where no one could see me or touch me. To get away from the pain and the humiliation. To no longer feel the self-loathing and disgust that I felt for not being strong enough to defend myself and my family. I just couldn't understand why they wanted to treat me that way, and why I was the one they picked on. After school when I got home and saw my mom and how beautiful and kind she was, I would wonder how they could say the cruel things they did about her.

Another time, an older boy grabbed me, pinned me against a wall, and fondled me. The look in his eyes will be forever imprinted in my brain. He reminded me of a lion that has just cornered its prey and knows there is no way it can escape. I believe his aim was power and not sexual gratification, but that didn't change how it affected me. It all happened so quickly and so unexpectedly that I didn't even have time to react. I just simply don't know how to put it into words how that moment affected me. I felt helpless, hopeless, humiliated, embarrassed, and very alone. These emotions all bounced and crashed around in my head all at the same time. What's worse is that some of the older boys saw it happen. It made me feel that I had been laid bare for the whole world to see and had done nothing to defend myself. If I had any self-esteem left at that point, that completely destroyed it. After that, I believed the only way to survive the onslaught of emotions was to become numb to them and completely block them out. As I began doing that, I slowly lost my identity. I became very adept at becoming whoever I thought the people around me wanted me to be.

The bullying wasn't just my getting tied to posts or pushed up against walls. It also happened at mealtimes. As poor as we were at the time, we didn't get very many store-bought snacks in our lunchboxes. I distinctly remember watching other kids eat their snack cakes and chips and wondering how it would feel to not have the same thing day after day, to never have to worry about food. Watching other kids eat made me think their lives were perfect. Sometimes they would trade with each other for certain snacks, but nobody ever asked to trade with me. Worst of all, I knew that I was being ungrateful. This realization only made me feel more awful about myself because Mom and Dad were doing their best to keep us clothed and fed, which couldn't have been easy.

Once, Mom had gone shopping and gotten fresh grapes for us—a treat! She let us eat some for dessert but told us to leave some for our lunchboxes. The next day at school, I was sitting on my lunchbox eating my sandwich when somebody kicked it out from underneath me. The lid flew off, and my food went flying. I had almost gathered everything back together when it got kicked again—and again. The lid came off my peaches, which scattered in the dirt. My precious bag of grapes landed right beside a kid, and I watched in silent anguish as he stomped them to a pulp. All that remained was my dirty sandwich, which I didn't feel like eating anyway at that point. I went to bed that night and wept until my pillow was soaked on both sides. When I closed my eyes, I saw my dirty peaches and smashed grapes.

Another thing I hated was getting spat on—a feeling so disgusting that it's hard to find the words to describe it. To have to wipe somebody else's spit off your clothes is so demoralizing and hurtful, especially if there is no explanation for it.

It wasn't just the lunch or the spitting; it was all of it at once, the bullying and the trauma together. Something inside me felt like it was dying. It hurt so bad. After listening to kids mock and demean me for so long, I started to believe them. I started to believe that I was stupid, ugly, weird, and warped. My grades started going down, and sometimes the teacher would spank me when my handwriting was bad. I couldn't concentrate. I wasn't sleeping well. I wet my bed. I was a mess.

I felt like I was unlovable. On our walk home from school, we would always pass Rachel's house, who was a beautiful girl with mental challenges. She would run out and hug my sister, and I've never forgotten the look in either of their eyes. They were so happy to see each other. I remember thinking that if somebody looked at me like that, I would have been the happiest kid in the world. It would take me years to realize that plenty of people looked at me like that, but I'd just assumed that those people didn't really know me. They were just being nice. For years, if somebody showed me love, I wondered what they wanted from me. I learned to watch people's eyes and facial expressions, and I became very adept at gauging feelings and emotions of others. That has never left me; to this day, I still watch people's eyes and read them. It's a tool of survival I learned as a child.

FINALLY, A FRIEND

I did start to make some friends eventually; it took a lot longer than I like to admit. I started collecting baseball cards and trading with some neighbors. We would sit in the front yard, arguing for hours about which card was more valuable and why the others should be willing to trade. I always looked forward to seeing them come up the road.

One year when Mom and Dad had communion church (all-day church with no kids involved), my friend asked if I wanted to bike to the city and visit the go-carts and batting cages. I couldn't believe it. Not only did I have a friend, but he was asking me to go with him! I had always dreamed of going, but there was one problem: I didn't have the money to go, or even a bike to ride there. He told me not to worry about the cost to get in, and he let me borrow his brother's bike. The night before, I raided the shoebox where I kept my treasures, putting my small stash of change in a Ziploc bag. The next morning, with the change in my pocket, I waited by the road anxiously, long before he was due to arrive. When we arrived in the city, he was true to his word; I didn't have to use my little bag of coins. I'll never forget the feeling of that first go-cart ride either. The wind whipping through my hair, the sun warm on my skin. It may sound small, but I really can't put it into words how much that day meant to me. For days afterward I would get a warm feeling thinking about it.

Looking back, I did have many trying times in elementary

school, and I was bullied horribly. In reality, though, it was only a small percentage of the kids who were bullies. As I reflect, I can also see how I may have brought some of the alienation on myself because I had a temper, and I was never sure how to communicate with other kids. That—coupled with the fact that I was a sad, lonely child who didn't trust adults enough to confide what was really going on—certainly colored my early relationships with my peers.

THE DOCTOR IN THE WHITE COAT

One memory from my early years that is prominent in my mind: when I was six, I had to have (another) surgery on my nose. I was born with a harelip, and the bone wasn't growing quite right. When I went in for my surgery, I was very nervous. I felt skittish around the doctors and nurses, especially because they did not speak my language (literally).

Before I went into the procedure, my mom tried to explain everything to me, but it wasn't enough. After they took me back, I tried to fight to go back out to Mom, but the nurses held me down. That's the last thing I remember.

When I came to, I was in a huge white room all by myself. Still scared and feeling very alone, I started crying for my mom. Out of nowhere, a doctor with long hair and a beard appeared and asked—in perfect Pennsylvania Dutch—what was wrong. When I told him I wanted my mom, he reached for my hand.

"Sleep now," he said, "and when you wake up again, your mom will be right beside you."

Though I have never trusted men, for some reason I trusted this strange-looking doctor completely. He held my hand until I fell asleep again, and when I woke up—just like he'd said—my mom was sitting right beside my bed. I told her I'd been afraid until the strange doctor who spoke our language told me she'd be there when I woke up.

After I told her the story, she and Dad tried to find the doctor to thank him. They asked the staff if there was anyone there who could speak our language. There wasn't.

I have always been sure that I know who it was. Maybe it was a white robe and not a white coat.

ON THE MOVE

We moved to Danville, Ohio, when I was twelve. It all happened suddenly: Dad came home with a flyer someone had put on his lunchbox describing a property for auction. It had a farmhouse with a barn, shop, creek, pond, and ten acres. My parents weren't sure if they would be able to afford it, but they decided we should go at least look since it was, after all, an auction.

I was unsure about the idea because I only had one year left in school, and the thought of starting all over scared me. Though I still wasn't happy and never let anyone get too close, things had gotten better at school. What swayed me was my cousin Bennie; his family had moved to Danville previously, and I couldn't wait to be able to play with him again.

Two Saturdays after he got the flyer, Dad was driving us the hour to Danville. It began to sink in that we might be moving away from our home and everyone we knew. When we arrived, the home had an empty look about it. The more I walked around, though, the more I began to see potential. Bennie reiterated my excitement at the thought that we might be close again.

When the day of the auction arrived, my parents dropped us off at Grandma and Grandpa's. My siblings and I were stir-crazy all day. We waited by the door for Mom, who smiled warmly and nodded yes when we bombarded her with our cries of "Did we get it?" I wasn't quite sure what I wanted: one minute I hoped we would get it, and the next I was afraid we would. But it didn't matter: the decision was made.

Thought it was hard on Mom to move that far away from her mom, dad, brothers, and sisters, she made the sacrifice for us. She knew we would have more room to roam, and I'm forever grateful for her unselfish decision.

School had already started before we moved, so we would be entering a couple weeks late. That fact made me even more anxious. I was a jittery ball of nerves that first day, avoiding eye contact with everyone. The first kid to break the ice was a kid about my own age named David. He suggested we play a game of dodgeball—which I won, repeatedly. Instead of being excited, though, I was terrified of their retaliation. Looking back, it's sad that I was afraid to win a game, but that was my mindset at the time. I finally realized that David and the others actually held no grudge. I had promised myself I wouldn't make any friends so I wouldn't get hurt in the end, but David made that very difficult. He was only a month older than me. He seemed to accept me for exactly who I was. Without even trying, he slowly coaxed me out of my shell. At first I was very wary of it all. At night I would lay in in my bed wondering what he wanted from me. I felt that sooner or later the hammer would drop and I would be back in my lonely little world, but that never happened. As time went on, we became very close friends and got into all kinds of trouble together in school.

Once, at an auction, a group of boys walked by and shoved me in the chest, sending me backward over a buggy shaft. In an instant, David was in the boy's face, threatening him with all kinds of bodily harm. I was amazed someone had stuck up for me and felt blessed to have a friend like that (though I eventually became good friends with Raymond, the kid who shoved me). That illustrates how, after becoming friends with David, it was easier to become friends with the other boys in school.

A HEARTBREAK, A PREMONITION

One day in Danville, I was watering the pony when two English boys walked up the driveway to ask if they could pet her. One of the boys, I learned, was Matt—and he had just moved in next door. We became fast friends.

He started coming over to our house every day, bringing his dirt bike. While we rode the dirt bike, he would ride the pony. His dad worked for Rolls Royce and traveled a lot, and his mom knew we didn't care if he stayed at our house. If he stayed over for a couple of days, he would wear our clothes, even wearing an Amish hat to go outside. He was so much a part of our family that when they moved back into town, it felt like one of my brothers had moved away.

Matt's dad was well known around town for being a wild child. That said, what I remember best about him is that he always stuck up for people who were weaker than him. He couldn't stand seeing people getting bullied. One time some Amish boys were getting bullied by some English kids, and Matt's dad happened to see it. He went to his car and got a baseball bat and threatened to put them in the hospital if they didn't leave immediately, which they did, knowing he would do exactly as promised. Matt's dad also drove a black Firebird that was probably one of the fastest cars in Knox County and would accept the challenge to race anyplace, anytime. It wasn't unusual to see him racing through town or doing burnouts on main street. At times it was almost like he had a death wish—and later it would turn out that he actually did.

Shortly after Matt moved back to town, we got word that his dad had committed suicide. It was very hard to believe that such an energetic, vibrant person was gone forever. It was tragic. I always wondered if he was bullied and maybe that's why he couldn't stand to see other people being treated that way. That really taught me that no matter how people act, look, or talk, we all have sorrow and pain in our lives. Some people are just better than others at hiding it. That doesn't mean it's not there. It just means we don't see it.

After Matt's dad committed suicide, we didn't see much of him anymore. He started to hang with the wrong crowd, and it wasn't long before he was heavy into drugs and drinking. It hurt to see the transition of such a carefree young kid turn into a zombie and lose all interest in anything that involved energy. We lost contact with him for a few years. I saw him once on the street in another town, and I almost didn't recognize him. It was so hard to see him and try to talk with him. I could tell his mind was somewhere else and he really wasn't my brother Matt anymore. Though it broke my heart to see him like that, I tried not to show it. I remember hating drugs and wondering why someone would take them if they made you act like that. Oh, how little did I know!

CHAPTER THREE

Choosing My Destination

Rumspringa and Coming Home

After I graduated, David and I didn't see each other very often anymore since we both got jobs and were both busy on most Saturdays. About the only time we saw each other was in church, which made it almost worth it. It was in church that I first laid eyes on the beautiful young lady who would later become my wife.

As soon as she walked in, David leaned over and whispered, "There is the girl you're going to end up with. You're going to marry her someday."

I laughed and shrugged it off. At the time, I didn't like myself and couldn't imagine a girl looking at me with anything but disgust. In my mind, a girl would have to lower herself just to be seen with me. I didn't know it at the time, but she saw David and me talking about her and thought we were making fun of her. Her family had just moved there from another community. Because she didn't know anyone, seeing us talking about her certainly didn't make her feel very welcome. If somebody told me that day that someday this sweet, innocent girl would save my life and bring me back from the brink of self-destruction, I would have thought they were losing their mind.

Eventually, I did take enough of an interest to find out her name was Esther, and I kept track of her for a while even though she started going to a different church. Then, life started to change, and my memory slipped. David started rumspringa a while before I did, so my weekends were spent working. When I started rumspringa of my own, I dove in, attending volleyball games with my friends and getting drunk with my buddies every weekend. It felt incredible to belong to a group, even though I was rebelling against everything I'd been taught. I even grew my hair down to my shoulders—something almost unheard of in the Amish community.

I received nasty comments for my hair, but instead of feeling bad about the ridicule, I embraced it—which also drove my parents crazy. At that point in my life, though, as long as I had my weekend buddies, I didn't care what they said. Since I felt included by a group of friends, I would do almost anything they asked me to. Nothing was too crazy or dangerous. There are two instances that still give me goosebumps when I think about what could have happened. It shames me to even share them, but if they can help another teenager going through this same thing, so be it.

First, one Super Bowl weekend, one of my buddies rented a limousine from a friend. There were eight or nine of us who helped pay for it. After the game and afterparty, we finally started for home. We had been drinking all afternoon, and none of us should have been driving. Nonetheless, I convinced my buddy to let me drive partway home. There was a lot of snow on the ground, and it was late. Long story short: I was driving a limousine down a back country road at seventy miles per hour with no lights, no license, no insurance, while drunk, and underage. The worst part is that I had eight drunk kids in the back with their lives completely in my hands. It makes me sick to my stomach when I think about what could have happened.

The second time, we were coming home from a concert. I had gotten my driver's license and bought a car, so I was driving. I usually drove pretty fast, and that night was no exception. Coming home on Route 3, I opened up and hit 110 miles per hour before I backed off and came back down to sixty-five. I didn't think anything more about it until the next morning, when I went started to drive to the gas station. Then, I saw my left rear tire: a spare I had put on two days prior, when I'd gotten a flat. A tire rated for only forty-five miles per hour. I was in shock that the tire hadn't blown when I hit such high speeds the night before—with my friends in the car, and everyone unbuckled.

At first, rumspringa was like this: all fun and games. Going to parties, drinking, and acting stupid was the only thing that I looked forward to, and I never considered the fact that it wouldn't last forever. Of course, things were about to change—and when they did, I didn't like it at all. The first big change came when a group of girls started rumspringa. Seemingly overnight, most of my buddies had girlfriends and didn't have time to hang out anymore.

I felt lost without my buddies and resented the girls. Shortly after, I started hanging around Esther's brother Marvin, who we all called "Snoopy" for some of his crazy antics related to his name. He had just broken up with his girlfriend. He was as aimless as I was at the time, so we clicked. He was older than I was, and though I never hung out with him much, I had always looked up to him. When he asked me one day if I could pick him up the following Saturday night, I was both delighted and surprised. After that, we started hanging out with each other on Saturday nights.

After a while, Marvin started teasing me about his sister

Esther, who was approaching rumspringa age. At first I pretended like I didn't even know which sister she was, but after a couple of weekends, he finally got me to admit that I thought she was cute. It wasn't too long after that that Snoopy asked me one weekend if I could keep a secret. After getting me to agree not to tell anyone, he told me that he was done with the Amish life and would be leaving the next weekend. It was a complete shock to me, though I tried hard not to show it. He had always seemed so carefree and happy with his life just as it was. It truly hurt me to know I was losing a good friend. He promised he would come and hang out with me on the weekends, but we both knew it probably wouldn't happen. The next weekend, I went into town to say goodbye only to find out he was already gone.

A couple of months after Snoopy left, Esther started rumspringa. My friends, remembering that Snoopy had told them I wanted to go on a date with Esther, asked her what she thought. To my pleasant surprise, she accepted. After that first date, we started seeing each other more often, and soon we were dating. I honestly didn't know what this sweet, innocent girl could possibly see in a broken, messed-up kid like me. I felt that once she saw who I really was, she would leave me in a heartbeat. I was so afraid of letting her in that I made a big mistake: I broke up with her, losing the best friend and companion I'd ever had.

When I broke it off with her, she took it extremely hard. I

tried to make her understand that it wasn't anything she had done. I told her I had issues that I needed deal with, but I just couldn't bring myself to tell her what they were. And, of course, she didn't believe a word of it. A normal-thinking person would have expected her reaction, but in my state of mind, I was actually surprised that she took it so hard. I had never had anybody outside of family grow attached to me before.

It was long buggy ride home that night. At this time, Mom was pregnant with my sister Ruth. I didn't want to stress her out with my problems, so I just did what I did best and suffered in silence, keeping the pain bottled up deep inside. I had taught myself to never cry, so I couldn't even do that. Instead, I sat on my bed for hours, thinking about what it would feel like to hold her in my arms one more time. I was so depressed that I considered what it would be like to go to sleep and never, ever wake up again.

Ultimately, I wanted to be away from everyone. But since that wasn't possible all the time, I started drinking more and more so I could become somebody else when I was with other people.

Soon, Mom had Ruthie. She was just what I needed at the time. I couldn't get enough of holding her every chance I got, marveling at her precious innocence. She was barely out of the hospital before we started calling her Tootsie. Holding her and looking at her tiny face, I so wanted a little girl of my own. I would think about how I would teach her how to swim and take her everywhere with me. To teach her how to tie her shoes and fix her hair. As she grew older, we teased Ruthie to no end, but we spoiled her even worse. I had her riding horses before she could walk. I carried her everywhere—so much so that Mom told me to stop because if I kept it up, she'd never learn to walk.

LEAVING THE AMISH

After Mom had Ruthie, I started thinking about leaving the Amish again. I had been thinking about it for quite a while already, but I didn't want to put more stress on her during her pregnancy. I finally made my decision, and I chose to leave without telling anyone. I should have realized that you can never run or hide from yourself or your problems, but that is a lesson I would have to learn the hard way.

After living with a friend for a couple of weeks, I moved in with my employer, Isaac, his wife, Britt, and their one-and-a-half-year-old baby, Liberty. They let me stay in their back room for free in exchange for babysitting Liberty. I didn't have to think twice: I missed Tootsie terribly, so it seemed fitting. I spoiled that little girl to my heart's content. Once, I was sitting in the living room with Isaac's wife, Britt, and Liberty hurt herself in the adjacent room. She came crying—running right past her mom—and straight to me. I will never forget how that made me feel, to have someone trust me with their problems.

Though I liked living with that family, I began falling back into my depression. No matter how fast I drove or what I did for a rush, it wasn't enough to keep me from feeling alone and empty inside. It didn't matter how many people around me loved me; I still felt unaccepted and alone. I considered moving back home, but I didn't really want to. At the same time, I wasn't happy where I was. In short, I didn't know what I really wanted out of life. The tipping point came one night when I went home to visit my family. When it came time to leave, Tootsie wouldn't let go of me. When Mom tried to peel her hands from my shirt, she started screaming and crying for me not to go. Before I drove away, I took one long look at the house. Tootsie was screaming and beating on the window with her little fists. That image is forever burned into my brain. I left, but I felt so horrible that I wanted to hurt myself. I couldn't stop thinking about how cruel I was to break her little heart like that. I absolutely hated myself and seriously thought that friends and family would be better off without me since all I did was hurt them anyway.

When I got home that night, Britt could tell right away that something was wrong. When she started questioning me, I ignored her. She was frustrated—rightfully—and told me that if I couldn't trust my friends or family with my problems, then eventually my problems would get the best of me. And—she said—nobody wants to live with somebody like that. Though her words stung, I needed to hear them.

Up to that point, I had hardly ever cried. I simply wouldn't allow myself to, especially in front of somebody. In that moment, though, when I felt myself getting teared up, Britt would not let me go outside. She grabbed me and gave me a quick hug. I completely lost it. It was as if a dam broke, and there was no way to hold back the water. For almost two hours straight, all the pain, frustration, loneliness, humiliation, and helplessness all came out in the form of tears. I felt ashamed to be crying in front of someone, but afterward I felt so much better. I slept better that night than I had in a long time. After I started crying, Britt just left me alone and let me cry in peace. This was the right thing to do at the time, as I wasn't ready to talk about it. The next day she questioned me about it, but I just told her that I was really missing my baby sister. Which was true—but not the whole truth. We both knew it. I never did tell her, actually, but just having someone I could talk to was enough to open the door. Right after this incident, I started to seriously consider moving back home to my family. I was restless and homesick and I really wanted to be there as Tootsie was growing up. I finally made up my mind to do it. When I told Isaac and Britt about it, they fully supported my decision, but they were both sad to see me go. We all knew that Libby would take it hard. It was so hard to say goodbye to my little buddy.

I felt bad to be leaving her behind, but I really needed to get back to my family. At first I saw her about twice a month, but as time went on, I saw less and less of her. I'm ashamed to admit that I haven't seen her in years.

CHANGING COURSE

I came home on a Friday, and it felt so good to be back. I relaxed that night, caught up with all the news, and got all the hugs and kisses from Tootsie that I had been missing out on. That Saturday night, I reconnected with old friends. Bennie and Esther's sister Emma were dating, and almost all my friends had girlfriends. A new group of guys had started rumspringa, and I started hanging with them on Saturday nights. Dad had nine acres of land about a quarter mile from where we lived. Often, on Sunday afternoons, we would meet there, build a fire beside the creek, and just sit around drinking and talking. Because Bennie was dating Emma, it was inevitable that I cross paths with Esther again. When I did, she was sweet as ever, and I stupidly tried to play it cool.

Since we both had friends in the same group, we saw each other almost every weekend. As time went on, we started spending more and more time together—just us. We were both more relaxed and mature than the first time around. Months later, the night before Valentine's Day, I finally gathered up the courage to ask her out. Her acceptance blew me away.

I had my family, and I had Esther. I was home, and this time I wasn't leaving.

CHAPTER FOUR

A Lantern to Guide My Way

Marrying the Love of My Life

When Esther and I started dating again, we promised to tell each other everything and anything. We knew that if we worked together, we could get through anything. We agreed that if we were truly satisfied with what we had, then we had everything!

When I was in school, I thought I would have been so happy just to have snacks like the other kids. For years, I struggled with that concept: always needing just a little bit more money, a vacation, or whatever it was that grabbed my fancy at the time. I still struggle with it once in a while, but I remind myself that Esther is God's personal gift to me. As long as we have each other, we are rich. We may always be broke, but we will never be poor.

It was the same way I grew up: broke, but never poor. As a kid, it was harder to see, but it's plain as day looking back. I wouldn't change it for anything. Esther and I knew we wanted our lives to be the same way.

After I joined the church—which means I committed to the Amish lifestyle post-rumspringa—I started working on buggies in my spare time, which slowly grew into a full-time job. At first, it was just a side job, and I only worked on them in the evenings and on weekends. As time went on, though, I started getting pretty busy. Eventually, I went full-time, though I found I was only busy in spurts—slammed one week, and nothing much to do the next. So, I began buying buggies at auctions, after which I would fix, repaint, and resell them. My goal was to have my business well established before Esther and I got married—something we already knew we wanted.

It was hard to imagine getting married, and I had so much to think about that sometimes it was hard to fall asleep at night. I would lay there in the quietness of my room and think about moving out and not seeing my siblings every day. But at the same time, I loved Esther, and knew that I wanted to spend my life with her. One night there was a full moon, and I just couldn't sleep. I couldn't believe that I had actually found someone who seemed to accept me the way she did. It is still amazing to me. In the light of the moon that night, I wrote her a poem. When I gave it to her, her reaction really surprised me. She almost cried! At first I was afraid I had crossed some kind of line, but she was quick to assure me it was very special to her. Though this makes me a little self-conscious, Esther wanted it in this book because it means so much to her, so here it goes:

Tonight as I lay looking at the moon. I can't stop my thoughts from drifting to you. Thinking about the one I love, the one I cherish. Hoping our dreams become true and flourish. Being together through good times and bad. Never to be lonely, never to be sad. The love I see when I look into your eyes. I hope and pray it never dies. When I look at you I feel a stirring deep inside. I think to myself, my heart hasn't lied. So tonight when you look up and see the moon. Please think of me. For I'll be thinking of you.

I must have written it at the right time because back then, Esther was going through a rough patch. Knowing how I truly felt about her helped. I always loved that we could talk about anything that was bothering us—or anything that wasn't, for that matter. We used to sit and talk for hours and hours about everything from how our kids would look to the weather. We told each other everything—with one exception: I did not tell her I had been abused. To be honest, I had repressed those feelings and memories so deeply that I'm not sure I could have if I'd wanted to.

While Esther and I were courting, we learned a lot about each other. For instance, she learned I have always had a serious battle with depression in the winter. It starts in the fall and just keeps getting worse as the months creep slowly by. By March, usually I'm struggling to keep it together. I always know that I should be glad that I can still hear the trees snapping from the cold, taste the cold fresh air, and see the fresh layers of snow, but it is so hard to feel that way after a few months of it. In the winter, I see three colors: black, white, and gray. Esther, the sweet woman that she is, knew this about me early and married me anyway. Can you imagine? But, we had agreed: we could get through anything.

To make matters worse, that particular winter, the old gang had all gone their separate ways. I hardly saw Bennie anymore, and several others had left the Amish. It seemed like Esther and I were the last ones left. We had been a close-knit group, and it was sad for me to think about all of us growing up and going our separate ways.

THE WEDDING

Despite how it may sound, I was incredibly excited leading up to our wedding. In fact, the last month before we got married went by so fast that I didn't really have time to think about what was going on. I was always rushing around getting this or that ready, or else I was on the road running errands. It was hectic, especially for Abe, Esther's father.

Finally, the night before the wedding, I had time to take a breath. I was staying at Abe's for the night. As I stood by the barn there, watching the sun go down over the hills, it struck me hard that I was actually getting married. I had thought about it a lot, but it seemed so surreal now that it was actually happening. As a younger teen, my self-esteem had been so shot that I had never even imagined a girl would ever look at me without disgust. I'm ashamed to admit it, but I used to hate to look into mirrors because it made me sad. Once, when I was still in school I overheard a girl say, "Even a blind person wouldn't kiss that ugly harelip." That one hurt for a long time, and to this day I won't put up with it if I hear a kid getting called stupid or getting bullied. It takes me back to those days, and that's not a place I want to be.

That night, standing at Abe's, I wondered how I had gotten so lucky. I felt blessed that I had found a beautiful, compassionate girl who loved and truly cared about me. To think that we would be spending the rest of our lives together was absolutely amazing. On one hand, I was excited and almost couldn't wait. On the other hand, I knew what a huge responsibility it would be, and I was extremely nervous that I wouldn't be up to the task.

That night, I almost couldn't sleep. October 16 dawned clear and very crisp. Everybody was nervous and chattering away until people started to arrive, then nobody wanted to say a word. The ceremony was beautiful. To my surprise, I wasn't nervous as much as amazed. Even walking up the aisle didn't seem real. It wasn't until I sat in the buggy to go to the reception that I realized that, for the first time in my life, I was sitting beside my wife!

The rest of the day went by so fast it seemed like only an hour or two before people started heading home, though it was close to eleven o'clock before everybody was gone. The next morning, we all got up early to start cleaning up. Every time I asked Esther a question, I was amazed that I was talking to my wife.

Since Bennie and Emma were getting married the next week, we couldn't move into the basement right away, so we lived in one of the upstairs rooms. By the time their wedding was over, I was ready to have everything go back to normal. Once their wedding was over and we had taken all the tables, tents, and dishes back, I moved my repair shop over to Abe's shop. I didn't mind working in the bakery while Abe still had it, but the following year they asked if we would take it over. We talked about it, but I left the final decision completely up to Esther. She didn't mind taking over the bakery, but only on the agreement that we could move out of the basement. Since we almost had to live right there, she got Abe to agree that we could build a small house on their property.

Once we took over the bakery, it wasn't quite as fun anymore, partly because it involved getting up at two o'clock in the morning to work the mixer—but we made it work, just like we promised each other we would.

DREAMING OF CHILDREN

Before we were married, we had often talked about having kids and raising a family. Esther always wanted a big family, and I would have been content with two or three children. As long as I had one little girl, I didn't care so much about the numbers. However, as the months went by—and then a full year went by—without kids, we began to suspect something might be wrong. We talked about going to the doctor, but we decided to give it a little more time. I think part of the reason we waited was because we were both scared to know for sure.

As time went on, it wasn't just me and Esther who were wondering if something was wrong. In the Amish community, everybody knows everybody, and most couples have kids in the first couple years of marriage. We didn't fit that mold—something the community noticed very quickly. The longer we didn't have kids, the harder it was on Esther. She dearly wanted to hear little feet on our floor, but it just wasn't happening.

I heard remarks about my not being "man enough" to have kids quite often, and there were a few times these statements hurt so badly that I almost couldn't take it. Esther would ask me what was wrong, but I just couldn't open up. A couple of times I started to, but I couldn't quite get it out. It was a mistake to keep it all bottled up because it made me feel alone and led to deeper frustration and temper issues. To be honest, at one point in time, I heard comments about my not having children almost every day, and it broke me.

What's worse is that, just like with the insults of my childhood, I heard these comments so many times that I started to believe them. The one thing that Esther wanted so dearly, so badly, was the one thing that I simply couldn't give her.

One day, I was finally able to tell her what had happened, what had been said to me over the past couple of years. She was shocked, and she couldn't believe I'd been carrying around that burden all alone. We cried together when I started telling her what had happened, and it all started coming. Everything that had been said to me over the past couple years came out. To say that she was shocked is an understatement. She couldn't believe that I had kept everything bottled up and carried that burden all by myself that whole time. We both cried together for a while and got it out of our systems, and though it still hurt, it felt good to share my pain with her. I told her that I would never help at the auction—the place where the men almost always seemed to torment me—ever again. She talked common sense to me, so eventually I agreed to go back—though I was very self-conscious.

At that time, we still hadn't gone to the doctor, and my desire to do so was waning. I was afraid the problem would be mine, and what the men said would be true. Plus, without knowing, we were able to cling to that tiny thread of hope.

That said, I put my pride aside, and we both decided to get tested—but it never happened.

The drugs hit, and it was all downhill from there.

CHAPTER FIVE

A Steep Downhill

My Slide into Addiction

Shortly after Esther and I got married, the economy took a big hit. Things became pretty tight financially in our young marriage. I was still doing business in the shop, but I was mostly just selling parts.

Many customers only wanted parts and did the work themselves, cutting down on the labor price. I completely understood this because times were tough for everyone, but that meant I wasn't bringing in enough money to support us. At the time, my brother was working at Mt. Eaton Pallet and said there may be a job available. I talked to Abe about it because I knew if I got a regular job, they would have to help in the bakery. Always supportive, he said if I had found a job with the economy the way it was, I should take it.

Taking the job at Mt. Eaton was a wonderful experience. I made many friends there, including Roy. He and I both loved horses and had worked around them, at one time or another. In fact, that's all we talked about. At the time, I was looking for a pony cart so I could train Abe's pony for him. I had been working with the pony for a while and had it trained to ride, but I needed a pony cart to train it to drive. When I asked Roy if he knew anybody, he grinned and said he had one for sale—on one condition. If I bought it, I would have to take the pony that came with it. Of course I was very suspicious, and wanted to know what was wrong with it. He laughed and told me that it was a very ugly color and was almost blind. He had worked with her a little bit, but she was hard to handle and she just acted strange sometimes.

That night, Esther and I talked about it. Though she was pretty skeptical about the pony, we both wanted the cart. We decided that we could always get rid of the pony if I couldn't train her. We arranged pickup for that Friday night, thus starting quite the adventure. The pony was indeed ugly, but I took my shot at training her.

I discovered the pony wasn't fully blind, but she was strange. She would stare at nothing and then take off, stop—and do it all over again. It was entertaining as long as you weren't riding her. I couldn't sell her as long as she acted like that. It just wasn't safe. Esther was always very worried about me and that pony, but like always, I thought I had everything under control.

In the blink of an eye, everything changed.

THE ACCIDENT

That night, everything started off as it had a hundred times before. I was always wary of the pony's craziness, but I was starting to hope that she was coming around, as she hadn't thrown any fits lately. Everything was perfectly fine—until I started to climb off. I was swinging my right foot out of the stirrup, when she went ballistic.

I have no idea how long she drug me around. The first thing I remember is Esther screaming at me, and it seemed like she was far off. I must have blacked out again because the next thing I remember is her being on her knees and asking me something. I thought I should answer, but I couldn't remember the question.

WHEN IT ALL STARTED: ADDICTION

Something hit me in the side of the head, and all I saw was a bright flash. I felt myself going limp. I felt my fingers slipping off the pommel, and I knew I was going down hard. In the back of my mind, I realized my left foot was still in the stirrup. But I was powerless to move. Everything was so hazy, except for one moment I remember with absolute clarity: as the pony was bucking around in circles, I looked up at the bottom of her stomach. As she whirled over top of me, I thought, "I wonder where my leg is at?" That one picture is so clear even to this day. It seemed as if time completely stopped. Then I blacked out.

When I woke up, the pain was so great that I thought I might have broken my back. Two weeks later, the doctor would prescribe Percocet.

It was the beginning of the end.

I hurt all over, but the worst pain was in my hip and back. It hurt just to breathe. When I was finally able to sit up, I realized nothing was broken. Other than that, I don't remember much from that night. If Esther hadn't seen what was happening, I don't think that you would be reading this book.

Esther put the pony in the barn and then helped me to the house. After rechecking myself for broken bones and not finding any, I took a shower and went to bed. I didn't feel like doing anything and would have been too sore, anyway. The next morning, Esther helped me out of bed and helped me get dressed. I was so sore, it was unbelievable. Since I didn't think any bones were broken, I didn't want to go to the doctor. I figured that the pain would eventually go away if I took it easy and didn't do anything too crazy. The soreness did gradually go away, but the pain in my hip and back never subsided. I couldn't get comfortable and wasn't getting much sleep as a result.

A couple weeks later, I caved and decided to go to the doctor. The X-ray showed no broken bones, so they set me up for an MRI the following week. In the meantime, though, he said he would give me something to help me sleep. He gave me a prescription for something called Percocet and told me to take them to sleep. He also instructed that if I got too uncomfortable during the day, I could take one or two. Looking back, it chills me to the bone to think I didn't know what those little pills could do. I don't want to blame the doctor, but growing up in an Amish home, I didn't know the first thing about drugs. I assumed if he said to do it, I should do it.

And he was right—I slept so well that night that I thought it must be a miracle. I felt great the next day and was able to work at full speed again. By that night I was pretty sore again, so of course I took another one. It wasn't until a couple of days later that I took my first one during the day. About fifteen minutes after I took it, I began to feel relaxed and energized at the same time. Everything was just so beautiful. The sun was bright, the birds were singing, and everything was going perfectly. It felt great just to breathe and be alive. A while later, it was a different story. I felt like I should go take a nap—drowsy and irritated. At that time, I still didn't realize that it was the pills that made me feel great or the crash that made me feel terrible. For me, that is what made these pills so seductive. I had always thought that if you took drugs, you would get an almost instant high. It didn't work that way. They would slowly kill the nerve endings until there is no pain or feeling left except pleasure. It would just come across me slowly. I would feel the muscles in my neck start to relax and know what was coming. It didn't matter how bad my problems were or how badly I was feeling. If I took a pill, I knew that in the next couple of minutes, everything would be alright—and I mean *everything.* Because of the emotional abuse, I had always felt that I was different and felt like an outcast. But when I took a pill, all those worries disappeared too. For the first time in my life, I felt fine just being me. I felt totally at ease anywhere, anytime. That was a huge problem for me because pretty soon I was taking them whenever I knew that I would be around a lot of people.

For the first time in my life, I didn't mind going to church. In fact, I looked forward to it! It was amazing how much those pills helped! Anytime I had a problem or someone said something that hurt me or that I took the wrong way, I just took another pill. It was a pick-me-upper I depended on. That following week, I went in to do the MRI. Once again, they didn't find anything damaged. The doctor asked me if the pills were helping me. I said yes, but that I was almost out.

He gave me another prescription, but this time it was for Oxycodone.

These weren't as strong as the Percocet, but they are still an opioid and work the same way. He made an appointment for me to see him in three weeks and gave me enough to last until then. At first, I took them as needed, but it wasn't long before I was taking them because they made me feel good. The next step was to take two at a time. If one made me feel so good, I reasoned, imagine what two would do!

Then three.

Then four.

But only at bedtime. At that point, during the day, I would only take the pills as needed. That's what I told myself, anyway. At first I saw him about once a month; the doctor simply started dropping off the prescription at the pharmacy for me to pick up.

It wasn't long before I realized that I wasn't going to have enough to last the month, so I had to cut back on my intake. To say that I got irritated and grouchy is a huge understatement. My poor, sweet, little lady got the brunt end of it all. Looking back, how I treated her hurts so badly. I honestly don't know how she was able to go through all that without losing her mind. She is by far the strongest person I have ever known.

I'll never forget the first time that I truly snapped at her for absolutely no reason: she had come out to the shop to ask me a question, and for some reason, I flew off the handle. Her stunned and hurt expression is etched into my memory. After she went back into the house, I stood there, angry at myself for having treated her that way.

I would love to be able to say that from then on, I thought before I spoke and that I never talked to her like that again. But the sad, painful truth is that the longer I was on those pills, the worse I got. By the time I went to rehab, that was my normal way of talking to her. I can talk for days about how good those pills made me feel, but what is so hard to talk about is what I did when the effects wore off.

Only later, in rehab, would I learn what was happening inside my body. They explained it like this: the dopamine level in your brain controls your moods. If something good happens, your dopamine spikes, helping you forget pain and stress and leaving you feeling light and happy. The highest dopamine can spike naturally—without the help of drugs— is 200 percent above normal. The counselors in rehab told us that the only time this happens is when a woman has her first child, and they place the baby on her chest.

The drugs—specifically, the amount of drugs—I was taking was causing my dopamine to spike up to 1,200 percent. Think about that for a moment: I was feeling almost one thousand times better than a woman who had just given birth and was meeting her baby for the first time.

The rush I felt on drugs was something I can't even describe. My family and friends didn't understand why I couldn't just quit, but if you think about the dopamine rush I just described, it just wasn't that easy.

The worst part was coming down. If a woman's dopamine level spikes that high when they place the baby on her chest, imagine what would happen if they took her baby away and told her she could never have the child again? What would she do to get that baby back? She would probably think about her little baby a thousand times a day, wondering what she looked like or how it would feel to hold her again.

Add 1,000 percent to that longing, and that's how I felt about my pills. I know it sounds brutal, but the harsh reality is that mothers and fathers give up their children every day because of addiction. People trade their lives for it. I almost lost my wife and everything that I had for it.

The worst part about the drug is that it actually helps you justify almost anything in your own mind, and you don't even realize that's what's happening. The brain is trying to survive, and the drugs tell your brain it needs them to survive. It will do almost anything to survive, and the drugs tell your brain that you need them to survive.

To illustrate this point for us in rehab, they discussed a study that was done on rats. Researchers placed a lever inside their cages that, when pushed, gave them drugs. Within two days they were addicted, and by the third day, they were no longer eating or drinking. Instead, they stood by the lever—pushing and pushing. In the end, the rats starved to death, even though they had food and water in their cages. Their brains told them they needed the drugs the lever supplied to stay alive, so they pushed the lever until they died. Their last pitiful movements were pushing that little lever. That is the terrible beast that is opioid addiction.

I understand what those rats felt like. It doesn't matter how high you get. When you come down, that's how far down you are going. Imagine being 1,000 percent more depressed than a normal person would get. And the only way out? More pills. It's a vicious, heartless cycle that leads to severe mood swings. These mood swings are what make it so difficult for loved ones to understand or be able to judge how you are that moment—or how you'll be the next.

This dynamic was so unbelievably hard on Esther. She never knew which husband she had at any given moment. One moment, I would be happy, excited, and filled with energy and love. The next instant, I would fly off the handle for no reason at all and without any warning. She didn't know how to help, but she tried. In fact, it truly breaks my heart to think of how hard she tried to please me or do special things for me during this time, and I treated her like absolute crap. If I didn't outright ignore her, I'd destroy her plans. Looking back, I see I wasn't just destroying myself, but I was dragging her down with me. I see now that we were just a couple of naïve young kids. There was no way to know in the beginning that my beautiful wife would put up with my behavior.

My addiction started slowly, and I didn't realize I was digging a hole for myself. It was Bennie who told me it was possible to become addicted. Before that, both doctors I asked told me that as long as I had pain, I'd be fine. One doctor told me not to worry about what other people said about the pills; if I needed them, I should take them. I hung onto those words for a long time. When anyone tried to tell me they were afraid I may end up addicted, I told them the doctors had told me it was fine. I told them the doctors said that as long as I was in pain, I should take them. Of course I was in pain back then. In rehab, they explained that as your brain becomes addicted, it tells your body it's in pain in order to keep getting the drugs. It's telling that after I got clean, my back pain "went away."

Over time, my body became used to the drugs, so I had to take more to get the same high. Then, I took them simply to function. I was in a place so dark that I was willing to end it all just to get away from the pain. At my very lowest, suicide seemed like a relief, a way out. Nothing was fun anymore. I had no energy or will to do anything at all. I hated how I was treating Esther and figured she was better off without me, anyway.

It hurts for me to think about, it but it took me almost six years to hit the absolute bottom. But not before I put my sweet little lady through some of the worst sorrow possible. I was still working at Mt. Eaton Pallet at the time, and I had a good thing going. I had friends and enjoyed my work. As my addiction worsened and my pill intake grew, though, I started losing my temper more and more, until even my closest friends weren't sure about me sometimes.

At that point, I had started taking far too many pills. Once, I started bleeding from my mouth for no reason at all. That scared me and should have woken me up, but it didn't. Then, my company transferred me to a different position, and I lost it. I didn't want to work with anyone else. I was already spending a lot of money on pills, so to compensate—and rather than cutting back on my pills—I decided to get a higher paying job so I could afford them.

We had just bought a new place next to my brother-in-law's home, and it was Esther's dream home. It was set back in the woods with complete privacy. To me, though, I was at the point where I didn't really care about anything except my pills. I looked at it as just another home. My poor little lady had all these grand dreams about us living alone together for the first time in our married life. She wanted a big garden and a small orchard with apples, pears, grapes, and berries. Sadly, I shattered her dreams one by one. Those dreams cost money, and of course the pills were much more important to me. She got a job teaching school to help with the financial problems, but it didn't help at all. I just had more to spend on pills.

I was ready for another job almost as soon as I didn't get to work with my friends at Mt. Eaton anymore—which was one of the worst decisions I could have made. I loved the work, and the pay was great—but the place had a river of drugs running through it. I worked in the parts department, which brought me into contact with everybody in all departments. I had total freedom to walk around the shop at any time. If I needed something to get me through the day, I would roll some dollar bills together, grab a part off the shelf, and go visit somebody. It was crazy how available and easy drugs were to get there. I had been taking a whole bunch of my own pills at a time up to this point, but now I had *options*.

My big mistake was buying some Perk 30s (Percocet 30 milligrams). My prescription was for 5 milligrams. A Perk 30 was almost six times what I had been taking. I had to pay almost thirty dollars per pill for 30s, which is a dollar per milligram. At the time, that was street value. After taking some of these, my prescription pills weren't nearly strong enough. To compensate, I just took more of mine to get the same high.

And then more.

And then more.

When I went to rehab, a doctor told me that I was taking enough painkillers to kill a major cancer patient. When I told him that I only had one kidney, he couldn't believe that I was still alive.

Eventually, a couple of jobs and some more money troubles later, I finally had enough to go into town to pick up my pills. I was pretty excited about having a full bottle again. And to top it off, it was Friday night! It was definitely going to be good weekend! I was happy when I got back home with my precious little bottle. There was Esther, standing in the kitchen archway. After watching me for a minute, she said, "You know, if you ever looked at me the same way you looked at that bottle of pills, I would be the happiest girl in the world." Then she turned away, sadly, and went back to the kitchen.

Up to that point, if something hurt me or I felt depressed, I would take more pills and it would go away for a couple of hours. This time, that didn't work. It didn't matter how many pills I took or what I did, I couldn't drown those words. I kept hearing them over and over. I had never stopped to think about what my pill use was doing to her. It was all about me and the pills. After she said that, I started going straight for the bottom. I simply couldn't take enough pills anymore. I tried everything to get those words out of my head. I started snorting the pills. Sometimes I would crush them and mix them with codeine. The first time I tried that, I woke up four hours later on the basement floor with no idea how I had gotten there. I even snorted methadone, which almost nobody does because it burns so badly. With everything I was taking, I still couldn't get high anymore. Nothing worked. I couldn't focus. I was barely functioning. My temper was always simmering right underneath the surface, and I would go off for any reason whatsoever. The world I was living in was so dark and depressing that I just didn't want to live in it anymore.

One Saturday afternoon, we were over at our new house—the one I'd bought because it was cheaper—doing some work. I don't even remember what went wrong, but something obviously triggered me. I just simply couldn't take being awake anymore. I let out a string of cuss words and smacked my head into the wall as hard as I could. It didn't knock me out as planned, but it knocked me flat on the floor. This just ticked me off more, and I sat up and threw myself backward as hard as I could, smacking my head on the floor again and again. A couple of times, I hit hard enough that my body from the neck down went completely numb, but no matter how hard I tried, I couldn't knock myself out. When Esther heard the thumping from outside, she came inside to see what was going on. When she saw what I was doing, she screamed my name and came running over. She got on her knees and held my head in her lap so I couldn't do it anymore. All alone in that big, empty house, we stayed in that position and cried for a long, long time. She stroked my hair, saying, "You need help, baby. We have to get you help." I get tears every time I think about that moment. I promised Esther that day that I would get help. I truly felt that I was beyond help, but I would at least make the effort. Esther got an appointment for me at SpringHaven Counseling Center in Mt. Eaton.

When she told them about the drugs and depression, they wanted to see me right away. They evaluated me and recommended a place called Glenbeigh Rehabilitation Center in Rock Creek, Ohio. The only problem was that it was quite expensive. It would cost around fourteen thousand dollars—not including the trips for Esther to come and see me on the weekends. I would be going through a one-month program. They recommended two months, but I just couldn't see taking off work that long. We started talking to family and friends about it, and word got around that I would probably be going to a rehab facility.

At the time, some of the comments about my plight cut pretty badly, and I came very close to not going. But I had promised Esther, and I wasn't going to go back on the promise. Part of me believed those people who said I wasn't worthy of their help, though—another reason it was so hard for me to go to my bishop, Reuben, and tell him I needed the church to help me pay for my problem. That was so hard to do. But admitting that I had a problem was really the first step in getting help.

The night that I went to talk to Reuben, I was incredibly nervous. I didn't know of anyone in the Amish community who had ever needed help with drugs before, and I wasn't sure what to expect from him. As I said before, I was always watching for people's reactions. That night, I told myself that if I sensed he thought I should pay for it myself or just borrow the money, I wasn't going to go through with my promise.

But that didn't happen.

I will never forget his reaction when I told him my problem. He didn't hesitate or flinch. He just said that if I wanted help, then he and the church would help me. He could have said that he wanted to gather more opinions or to talk to some other people, but he didn't. Before I left, he told me to just get better and not worry about the money. That it would all be taken care of. I knew that he would have to tell the church what was going on, but he assured me not to worry about it, that he was sure everybody would understand. It's hard to explain the relief I felt at his reaction. To know that somebody outside of family was standing firmly behind us went a long way toward helping me believe that I was making the right decision.

We had church at our house the Sunday before I left for rehab. Almost everybody in church that day came up and wished me luck. As they promised to pray for me, I felt touched and guilty all at once. I didn't feel right that all these people were paying out of their own pockets to put me through rehab. After I got clean, I would remember all these people whenever I wanted to take pills, and remind myself how many people I would be letting down if I relapsed.

The day before Esther and her mom, Katie, were taking me to rehab, I made sure that I had plenty of pills for the long ride up to the rehab center. I didn't want to show up sober. I was going to be as high as possible when I got there. On the way up, I popped ten pills: five when we started off, and five an hour later.

CHAPTER SIX

The Hardest Hill to Climb

Rehab

I had never been in a rehab before, and I knew that I would be the only Amish person there. I had no idea what to expect, how people would react to me, or if I would be accepted. By the time we got there, I had a slight buzz from the pills I had taken—even then, it wasn't enough to make the nervousness go away.

It was incredibly hard to say goodbye to Esther and Katie. We hugged and cried, knowing it was for the best. I knew that in four days I would see Esther again at Saturday visiting hours, but I didn't know when I would see Katie again. As hard as it was for me to say goodbye, I think it was hardest on Esther. She felt like she was abandoning me, and none of us knew how I'd be treated.

ESTHER'S EXPERIENCE

First of all, I was so happy when they finally had an opening for Monroe. They told us they had a long waitlist, but thank God they got him in. I didn't realize how hard it would be to leave him there with complete strangers, in a place we had never seen before and knew nothing about. The nurse assured us that he would be fine, but I still felt horrible and sad to leave him. As we were leaving, I looked back and saw him just standing there, looking so lost and sad that I almost wanted him to come back home with us. But I also knew that he was high and he needed help. I knew that I would see him in four days, but it was still incredibly difficult not being able to talk to or see him during that time. I cried and prayed a lot.

The nurse took me on a tour and explained the rules before showing me to the hospital wing, where I'd be staying the first week so they could monitor my vitals and keep me on meds. The meds were to wean me off the painkillers and to prevent seizures as I was coming down. When they took me to my room and searched my belongings, I got a precious surprise: Esther had placed a little note for me in between each set of clothes. Each one had its own little message, telling me how much she missed me, how she would like to touch me again, that she was praying for me, and to stay strong. The nurse had to fight back tears, but I was still high enough that it didn't really hit me until later. When it did, it hit me hard. I read them over and over, wondering what she was doing.

When I got settled, the staff gave me a pen and notebook and encouraged me to keep a diary, if I felt up to it. Most of the time I didn't feel like it at all, but now I'm glad that I kept the diary. My mind was so altered from being on pills for so long that it didn't function properly anymore. At first, I would write all my words completely backward. It was so hard because I would have to check every word and make sure all the letters were in the right place. It was almost like learning to write all over again. I threw those pages away, but now I wish I'd kept them as an example of what drugs can do to the brain.

Later that first day, I asked if they allowed smoking. To my surprise, they did. I still had about half a pack left, so I went out to the pavilion. Stepping out was nerve-wracking. There were almost two hundred people there, and I knew I stuck out like a sore thumb. Plus, I was still high, so it was hard to mingle.

As it turned out, I didn't need to worry at all. Most of the people there were younger kids, mostly between the ages of eighteen and twenty-four. They were all curious as to why an Amish guy was there. As it turned out, 98 percent of them were there for the same reason that I was. I was barely out the door before I was asked a lot of questions. The first guy who approached me was Jimmie*, an outgoing

---

* Some names changed for privacy.

character who told me right away not to worry about being Amish. He said we were all here to get better. Others who saw us talking came up and joined the conversation. I felt a little bit like an animal at the zoo, but it was OK. I met a lot of new friends that night, and everybody made me feel comfortable and welcome.

When the nurses woke me up at six o'clock the next morning for my vitals, I had a thought: it was the first time in six years I hadn't taken a pill in the morning. The longest I'd been off the pills in those six years was twelve hours. That was about to change. It is very hard to explain how it felt or how horrible that first week and a half was. For six years I had been numb, both physically and emotionally. When those feelings start coming back, there is no way to control them.

I had no idea what was ahead of me or how unbelievably hard it would get. If I had known, to tell you the truth, I would probably have walked out. I told Esther later that I would die before I went through that again. It started with the shakes, and my skin felt so tight that I honestly felt that it might break. It was just my nerve endings starting to work again, but I didn't realize it at the time. I couldn't blink my eyes because my skin felt too tight. I don't know if it actually *was* or if it just felt like it, but it was awful. During that first stage, when I looked in the mirror before I left the room, my own reflection scared me: white as a sheet, huge eyes, sweaty and stringy hair. I was shaking and twitching uncontrollably. My muscles were so tight and cramping up that I just had to do a little shuffle to walk. I didn't want to leave my room but knew that I would have to, eventually.

I'd quickly learn that almost everybody went through that stage. In fact, some got the shakes so badly that they had to be in wheelchair. In that environment, everybody helped each other. When I had the shakes, a girl carried my coffee back to my room for me because I just kept spilling it.

Eventually, I got so used to seeing the shakes that they didn't bother me anymore. But I will never forget the first time that Esther saw someone with shakes while she was visiting me: we were sitting in the cafeteria, and the only other person in there was a girl with the shakes. Esther didn't see her right away, but when she did, her eyes became very wide. She leaned over the table and quietly asked me what was wrong with her. I was so used to it that I wasn't sure what she was talking about at first. When she told me that she was talking about the girl who was shaking, I just started laughing. Esther was very disturbed, telling me firmly that it was not funny. Esther asked why nobody was helping her. I explained that I wasn't laughing at the girl; I was laughing because I was so used to it and simply didn't notice it. I told her I had, in fact, looked exactly like that, and there was nothing anybody could do. I tried to explain to her that the girl was perfectly fine, but I could tell she didn't believe me. She asked me if I was sure that we shouldn't go for help. I tried to reassure her by telling her that we look out for each other—lighting each other's cigarettes, helping each other eat—but other than that, there was nothing that could be done other than get through it. Eventually, Esther said she couldn't take it anymore and suggested we go for a walk instead. Esther never forgot about that girl. She still talks about her sometimes.

When the shakes slowed down for me, I began extremely skittish and jumpy—strung tight as a fiddle string. When my nerves started to come back to life, I began having strange sensations. Sometimes, I would feel very cold for no reason. Other times, it felt like there were spiders crawling all over me. It drove me nuts when I was trying to sleep. Even a simple raindrop could give me sensations unlike anything that I had felt before. It's like when you throw a rock into a pond: when it hits, ripples spread out from the impact. That's how it felt on my skin. If a rain drop hit me, say on the arm, the sensation would spread out until I could feel that single raindrop on my entire body. This could be very confusing at times, especially because all my feelings and emotions that had been suppressed for so long now all came crashing back at once.

Imagine that you had all five senses—hearing, smelling, touching, tasting, and seeing—all mixed in a bag. Also mixed up in this bag are all your emotions: happiness, sadness, surprise, anger, fear, and disgust. Your brain isn't sure when to use them and in what order to use them, so it sends a lot of mixed signals. It seemed like it would just pick one out of the bag and say, "Hey, let's see what this one does!" Sometimes I would start crying for absolutely no reason at all, or I would laugh about something that really wasn't funny. I would feel happy or sad or both, and have no clue why.

The only good thing was that we all knew what it was like, and nobody said anything. My body had to learn how to send me signals again, to tell me what I needed. I remember one day I started feeling very sick and was going to skip lunch. It was mandatory that we were all in the cafeteria, even if we didn't eat, but that day I just couldn't. One of my buddies noticed that I wasn't there and came up to my room to get me. I told him that I was so sick I was afraid to get up. He sat down on the bed and explained that I wasn't sick. It was just that my stomach didn't know how to tell me that it was hungry, so it was making me sick until it got some nutrition. I wasn't in the mood for his little pep talk, and I didn't believe a word he said. I thought he just wanted me in the cafeteria so I wouldn't get into trouble. I told him in no uncertain terms that if he believed his own little story, he was off his rocker. But he just wouldn't give up, and finally I went to the cafeteria. I was so sick that by the time I got there, I just put my head on the table and tried not to throw up.

My friend had gotten some extra food for me when he went

through the line. After arguing with him for a bit, he finally got me to take a couple of bites. It was amazing how fast I felt better! I ended up going through the line twice for more food! Within minutes, I wasn't sick anymore. My buddy had to rub it in for a while that I hadn't believed him, of course. He was there for ninety days, and he took me under his wing.

FRIENDSHIPS IN AN UNLIKELY PLACE

Sometimes, my friend Kendra would offer me a couple cigarettes—which was helpful because I usually had to wait on Esther to bring them, and I didn't like to bum. For some reason, Kendra kept an eye on me. I loved that poor girl, and as time went on we grew close. She once told me that she didn't think she would live another year. She was slightly aloof and didn't let anybody get too close, but she was extremely smart. She always seemed hyperaware of her surroundings. Maybe that's because her story was such a nightmare: her dad started raping her when she was eleven, and a year later her brother started. She was hooked on drugs by the time she was thirteen, ran away from home at fifteen, started hooking to support her habit, and eventually got caught. After doing some jail time, she ended up back home. Her dad caught her stealing some of his drugs, beat her up, and she ended up back on the streets. When she got caught again, she got out of the jail time on the condition that she complete rehab and move back in with her dad. When I asked why she didn't tell somebody about the abuse, she just gave me a sad little smile and said, "Nobody would believe me. My dad knows who to hand the money. Nobody's ever going to touch him." I think about her almost every day. She gave me her number, but I've always been too scared to call. I'm so afraid that she is no longer with us. I like to remember her as I last saw her.

Another person that I loved dearly was a tiny little girl named Andrea. She was barely five feet tall and weighed ninety-three pounds. I thought it was funny because she ate so much. I asked her once how she stayed that small, and her response made me wish I hadn't asked. She said that from the time she was three, she had to fend for herself. Her whole family was addicted to drugs, and she had to feed herself or go hungry. She said she honestly couldn't remember not being hungry. Sometimes, she simply couldn't find anything to eat. Sometimes, her family would leave for days at a time, and she'd eat dog food. When I think of that beautiful little blonde-haired girl all alone, eating dog food, it makes me want to scream in frustration and helplessness.

Andrea was itty-bitty, and she had a huge personality. She always tried to make everybody feel included. She was filled to the brim with energy and couldn't sit still. In lecture, she was always squirming around in her seat. She never walked anywhere; she bounced. When she finished rehab and left, I felt lost for a while without her giggles to brighten the gloom. Out of all the kids there, I probably missed her the most when she left. One day in lecture, the speaker told us to look around at the whole room and the people sitting next to us. After we did as told, he said that statistics show that in one year's time, only two of us would still be clean.

When I went back a year later for their annual reunion, only me and three girls were there from that class. I had been hoping and praying that Andrea would be there, but she wasn't. I was heartbroken. I tried to tell myself that she just couldn't make it, but deep down, I know the sad truth. I just don't want to accept it. The only consolation was that Kendra was there. She had survived a year, after all! She gave me a big hug, and we talked for a while about all the missing kids. She gave me a whole list of people that she knew had fallen back into drugs, but she hadn't heard anything about Andrea. That was the last time that I went to the reunions. It just hurts too much.

Another kid I grew close to was Kevin. He was skinny, completely covered in tattoos, and had rings everywhere. At first, I wasn't too sure about him, but after I got to know him, he was a nice, quiet kid. One day, I asked him what his tats meant. He got tears in his eyes and said that they don't mean anything. He said he hated them, but he had to have them to survive, based on where he came from. He told me tattoos are how he knows who to be afraid of and who to watch out for.

Because of Kevin, I vowed never to judge anybody on

appearance alone. No matter how rough the exterior might look, there might be a scared kid hiding inside, just trying to survive in this cruel world.

It seemed like everyone had a sad story in that rehab facility. Out of all those kids, I think I was one of the few who had grown up in a stable household. One kid's sister gave him crack for his eleventh birthday then raped him. Another was a Crips gangbanger who showed me the bullet scars from when he was ambushed at fifteen years old, walking out of a McDonald's. I could tell two hundred stories like these—all from one little rehab center in a small corner of Ohio.

Despite the troubled backgrounds, I felt completely safe in rehab. We were all in the same boat. We didn't see the color of one another's skin. We didn't question someone's ethnic background or religion. We had one enemy we all shared: drugs. We were there to fight it, not each other. We could talk about what the drugs did or made us do, and everybody completely understood—something that would never happen in the real world. By the time I left that place, I was so sick and tired of all the talking that I wanted to scream, but I needed it. The first time I went to group counseling—which was required by Alice, my counselor—I passed out. Literally. The guys later told me that they had made sure I was OK then decided to let me be.

I couldn't have asked for a better counselor than Alice. She was a sweet, kind lady who didn't take crap from anybody. She had to be strong. She had six kids cooped up in a little room for two and half hours each day. Six kids who would much rather be doing something else.

It was during these sessions that I started realizing I wasn't alone in being molested and raped. I never said anything about it at the time because it was still easier to ignore the hurt than to dig into that wound, but it helped to know that I wasn't the only person this had happened to. I think it certainly would have helped Alice understand why the pills helped me so much, but I was still afraid to bring it into the open.

THE WORST DAYS

The sixth or seventh day of rehab was the worst for me. They had just moved me from the hospital to the dorm rooms when the restless leg syndrome set in. My legs would jump and twitch, making it impossible to hold still for any period of time. I got a little over three hours of sleep in three days. During the night, I walked the halls. Every once in a while, I would go to the courtyard and smoke a cigarette, but even then, it was hard to sit.

I was totally exhausted and very much on edge. When they started subsiding and I was finally able to get some sleep, I began having extreme nightmares. They usually involved trying to get high. Stabbing myself with heroin needles until the walls turned red with blood is about the only one mild enough that I feel comfortable writing here. I would wake up screaming, kicking, and punching. It was kind of embarrassing, but in the dorms it wasn't anything unusual. I asked my roommate if I screamed in Amish or English, and he said that I used both languages. That's how I know I dream in both languages.

The last phase was the sneezes. When I started sneezing, some guys told me that it was my head clearing up from everything that I had snorted. Others said that it was just a myth. I don't know which is true, but at any rate, they called them the dope sneezes. It sounds funny, but if you sneeze one or twice a minute for two days, it gets old. You can't even speak a full sentence.

TOO HARD TO BE AWAY

The way the facility worked, if your behavior was good and your counselors thought you were ready, they'd move you from the dorms to the house when there was space.

With all the people in the dorms, the phones were always full and I was never able to talk with Esther in the evenings. In the houses, there were only six people and two phones. That meant there was usually one line open—so, naturally, I wanted to get there.

I had only been in the dorms for two days when it came over the intercom that my counselor wanted to see me. When I got to her office, she looked at me for a minute then told me that she wanted to know what was wrong. I didn't know what she was talking about at first. She told me that she was getting a lot of feedback from the nurses that I wasn't playing volleyball or cornhole and that all I did was sit around. She told me that according to my profile, I loved sports and was always active. She said it was unusual for someone like me to be inactive. Then she started asking about Esther. She said that my profile showed that Esther was a key figure in my life and, according to the assessing counselor, Esther was the rock that I clung to when things got tough. She said, "I know that something changed between you two or you wouldn't be acting like this, and I need to know what it is." I tried to tell her that nothing had happened and our relationship was stronger than ever. She asked what we had talked about in our last phone conversation.

I told her that I hadn't talked to Esther in a couple of days because the phones were always busy. I told her that I really worried at night because Esther was alone, and if I couldn't talk to her before I went to bed, it was a lot harder to fall asleep. I would lay there wondering what she was doing or if she was alright. She let me talk for a while. Then, she said, "You truly love her, don't you?"

I immediately started crying. The counselor smiled and said,

"I thought that might be your problem." She told me to hang in there and that things would get better soon. I thought she was full of it, but I didn't say that, of course. I just went back out to smoke another cigarette. The next morning I was paged and told to go to assessment office. *Oh boy, what now?* I thought. But when I walked into her office, she was grinning. "Get your stuff ready. You're moving to a house!"

I couldn't believe it! I didn't even know that there was an opening coming up. She told me that she could tell that Esther and I had a special connection, as opposed to many kids who came in without strong connections back home. She said that she could tell that staying connected to Esther was essential to my recovery. Before I left, I gave her a hug. When I did, she started tearing up and said if I ever needed to call and the lines were busy, I could come by her office to use her phone. That meant more to me than anything else she did or said. I walked out of that office feeling like I was walking on air. I went straight to my room and had everything packed and waiting hours before it was time to move.

I left Esther a message as soon as I got into the house and gave her the new number. After that, I was much more at ease and comfortable. The guys in my house loved Saturdays because they knew that Esther would be coming and that she would bring cookies or fresh bread. Sometimes, her mom would send stuff along too. Those visiting hours were the only thing that kept me going during the week. Another thing that helped tremendously was that I started getting a lot of mail. You can't imagine how much faster the day went when I got cards and letters. At first, I would get a card or letter a day, then more and more, until I was getting five or six a day. I felt so guilty sometimes when I was waiting in line for mail and some poor kid was told that they didn't have mail. You could see their face fall. I hated walking down the hall with five or six letters and packages and coming face-to-face with a kid that I knew didn't have any family.

The worst one for me was a girl named Minah. We had become good friends. The first time she saw me with a handful of mail, she started crying. She apologized for ruining my mail time, saying it just hurt that nobody loved her like that. I gave her a hug and told her that I loved her, but she just backed away, shaking her head. "You have no idea how lucky you truly are," she said, crying again and running back to her room.

I felt horrible for her—but she was right. I had never really sat down and thought about how blessed I truly was. I had grown up in a nice house surrounded by brothers, sisters, and loving parents. I had a wife who loved me, along with my in-laws, and a church that loved me enough to pay my way through rehab. Too often I take all this for granted, and that should never happen. Sometimes it takes a wake-up call, and that was a big one.

Minah and I had an unlikely friendship. She was a Black kid from the ghetto and had a violent history. She had no family and went from home to home, crashing wherever she ended up. I was never really exposed to violence. And no matter where we were or what we were doing, we always knew that we had a warm and safe haven to go home to. None of this really mattered. For some reason, we just clicked and became very good friends. She could be absolutely hilarious and see humor in everything; on the flip side, she could be moody and lash out at any little thing. She never lashed out at me, but I saw her do it a couple of times to other people.

Once, one of my friends told me Minah had let it be known that if anybody said any disparaging words about my being Amish, she would put them in the hospital. When I asked her about it, she looked at me—stone-cold serious—and said, "Not to the hospital. I would kill them." I don't know why she felt that way about me, but it could have been that it just felt good to stick up for somebody other than herself for a change. We all want to feel loved and needed.

I found out later that a few months out of rehab, she was back on heroin. This is heartbreaking and makes me want to scream. I knew her for such a short time in this life, but she taught me a serious lesson in being thankful for all the people around me.

About a week before our release, we had to go through what

they call a "trigger group," which is a test where they trigger your addiction to see how you would react if it happened outside of rehab. If we failed, we had to stay longer. I asked some other people how to pass it because I did not want to stay another month. I wasn't sure what to expect, and I was very nervous. Whatever I thought I was getting myself into, the result was far worse.

I went in with about eight women and three men. They made us sit in a circle and told us to close our eyes until we were told we could open them. When they told us to open our eyes, I had a prescription bottle with five Perks in it right in front of me. They told us to pick up whatever was in front of us. When I picked that little bottle up and heard the rattle of the pills, I almost went nuts. I instantly broke out in a sweat, and for some reason, I was seriously pissed. The counselor asked how I felt, and I told them that I was mad because there were barely enough left to get me high. She told me that was how it controlled us: I was already thinking about who to call and where to get more. She made me shake the bottle again, and when I did, I almost lost it. I lost complete focus on anything around me, and the only thing I could see were those pills rattling around. Everything slowed down, and I can still see those pills rolling around in slow motion.

We all had our favorite drugs in front of us, and I will never forget the reaction of one of the other men. He was leaning forward with his elbows on his knees, staring at his little twist of heroin. There was actually sweat dripping off his face and onto the floor. The counselor had a syringe and she kept pulling the plunger out of the back. It made a little popping noise and every time it popped he would jerk all over. He kept it under control, but just barely. The woman right beside me had crack in her hand and she almost shut down too. I saw that she was barely breathing and reached over and put my hand in hers. She started squeezing so hard that I seriously thought she was going to break my hand. After a moment, she took a couple gulps of air, and I saw the muscles in her face and arms start twitching as she slowly relaxed. I knew then that she was fine.

I wish there were some way that I could explain how much control that these drugs have over the brain. If I could put it into words, maybe people who have never been addicted could understand, and I think it would help prevent addiction. But there's no way.

By the time we left the class, I had a severe headache and felt sick to my stomach. As we left the room, I just couldn't help but take one last look at my pills. My counselor told me that I had passed, which was a huge relief. I was so ready to go home and just be with my little lady again.

I was naive enough to think that rehab was the hardest part, and that it would get easier after I got out. It was actually the other way around. I could never in my worst nightmares have imagined how hard it would get.

CHAPTER SEVEN

Painful Twists

The Aftermath

When I saw Esther and her driver pull into the parking lot to pick me up, I was shaking with excitement. I had a lot of emotions running through me all at one time. I was so happy to be leaving, but at the same time, I was scared. I was also sad to leave my friends behind, many of whom I knew I'd never see again. It was almost like I was leaving a safe haven for the unknown. As we left, it was hard to imagine that it was only a month ago that I had been heading the other direction. I looked back until the hospital was behind trees and I couldn't see it anymore. We had gone only a little ways when, without thinking, I reached in my pocket for my bottle of pills. I didn't even realize what I was doing until I couldn't find them. That's when it really sank in that I didn't have any and would never in my life have them again.

That first year out of rehab, I honestly don't think that fifteen minutes went by that I didn't think about them. If something wasn't going my way, the first thing I did was reach in my pocket for a pill.

I had only been back for about a week when I messed up for the first time in a bad way. I was trying to move a big freezer by myself, and I got my hand stuck between the wall and the freezer. I struggled for a little bit before I was able to get free, losing some skin in the process. Furious, I turned around and punched the wall. I knew instantly I had broken something. I felt bones snap and watched the swelling start right behind my knuckles. Esther went up to ask if our neighbor would take me in to the urgent care, and she came right down. I didn't feel like talking about it, but I knew that they both wanted to know why I would pull a stupid stunt like that, both suspicious I was after some pills.

They made it very clear to the doctor that I was not to get any painkillers or narcotics, although I clearly had a broken hand. The doctor stated that I had an addiction problem and a temper problem, so I was just going to have to suffer this one out. I knew I deserved every bit of it, but I still don't know why they had to be so smug about it.

TEMPTATIONS

In those low moments fresh out of rehab, it got to the point that I didn't feel that it was worth living without the pills. There were some circumstances that only made it worse. I had only been out of rehab a couple of months when I was in town one day and came across one of my old dealers. He knew that I had been in rehab, so I didn't think he would even try to talk to me. Instead, we were right next to each other when he flipped something at me. "Catch!" Reflexively, I grabbed it in midair. "It" was a small bottle completely filled with Perks. I just handed it back and walked away— one of the hardest things I have ever done. I felt completely numb, but I could feel the sweat running down my back. Afterward I cried for a while and got the shakes, but for some reason, I never told Esther until much later.

Another time, we were headed to Kentucky for the weekend when we stopped at a truck stop to use the restrooms. As I was walking down the hall to the restrooms, a woman came out of the women's room and almost bumped into me. From the way she was dressed and looked, it was obvious that she was a prostitute. As she went past me, she brushed her hair back and gave me a lazy smile. As she did, I looked into her eyes and felt like somebody kicked me in the stomach. I knew beyond a shadow of a doubt what she was on, and it cut through my brain like a razor. I went on back to the men's restroom, but I couldn't even go anymore. All I could think about was what she had. Something came over me and before I could even rethink it, I went to find her. But she was gone. I looked everywhere for her, but she had simply disappeared. All I could think about the rest of the way down was how close I had come to getting that feeling one more time.

When we reached our destination, Esther took me to the side and wanted to know what was wrong. I hadn't been telling her how hard it had been lately. She was always so proud of how well I was doing, and I didn't want to disappoint her. I started getting the shakes and crying, so we went for a walk. I just poured it all out. I told her how hard it still was and how I didn't think I could ever get over it. When I told her about the girl at the truck stop and admitted that I had actually gone to look for her, she said something that really made me think. "You know what I think?" she said. "I think that she was an angel sent to test your willpower and you failed. From now on, if this happens, think about that!"

I still do think about that when I see someone who is on drugs—which is a lot. A nonaddict may not even understand how available and everywhere drugs are. Every time I went to town, I'd get triggered, even finding myself scanning the ground every time I was in a Walmart parking lot. I know how crazy it sounds, but I have taken quite a few pills that I found on the ground in parking lots. Sometimes they worked; sometimes they didn't. Any one of them could have killed me, but I felt that it was worth the chance. I once took six pills at once that I found in a hotel parking lot. They didn't do a thing, so I have no idea what they were. If they had been blood pressure pills, they would probably have killed me. With that amount, almost anything could have.

Because I was so triggered that first year, it gradually got to the point that I didn't even want to go out. I began isolating more and more. I never wanted to go out or do anything—except maybe kayaking. The river was one place that I could relax and completely let down my guard for a couple of hours. It was just me and the sounds of nature. Sometimes, Esther would go along, and that only made it that much better. We would talk about everything we were going through or had been through. For some reason, it so much easier to pour out my feelings when I was kayaking. We would always stop on a sandbar somewhere so that I could take a nap. I could sleep better on the hard rocks of a sandbar than I could at home in bed.

One cold winter day, I was feeling extremely blue. Around noon, I told my Esther that I couldn't take it anymore and I was going kayaking. My little lady looked at me and told me, in no uncertain terms, that she thought I had totally and completely lost it. It was fourteen degrees when I started off at three o'clock in the afternoon. There is one place in the river where the water is pretty rough, but it was low that time of year. I thought that I could make it through without getting wet. I didn't. I got soaked. I had dressed in layers, and when my clothes started freezing to the kayak, I knew it was time to do something about it. I pulled over at a cave that I had discovered on an earlier trip. After building a warm fire and making a makeshift clothesline with some branches, I stripped and hung my clothes over the fire. Although I was completely nude, the cave was warm, cozy, and filled with steam from my clothes.

Once back in warm clothes, I felt good and started off again. I had lost a lot of valuable daylight and I knew Esther would be worried sick—and she was. It had been dark for almost three hours before I finally got home. I wouldn't really want to do it again, but it was an experience that I'm glad that I had. There was a full moon that night, and everything was bright and glittering. My paddles got heavy with ice and they flashed in the bright moonlight. The water looked completely black, reflecting everything. In the summer nights, you can hear all the frogs, crickets, and night birds. Not that night. I have never in my life heard such deep silence. It was absolutely, completely silent. Every once in a while, the river would gurgle, but other than that, it was totally quiet. It was quite an awe-inspiring experience.

The bad part about kayaking was that I was never ready to go back to all my problems. In fact, being out in nature like that always helped me for a while, but it seemed to help less and less as time went on.

SLIPPING INTO DEPRESSION

I was slowly winding up like a spring, and it was only a matter of time till it let loose and everything came crashing down. Every time that I lost my temper or wanted some drugs, I felt so bad because I would hurt Esther in so many ways. I got to a point that I didn't feel that I could ever make it up to her. It seemed that the harder that I tried, the more that things didn't work out. Since I tried so hard to get it right, when something went wrong, it tended to hurt even worse. I was going around in a vicious circle that got worse every time I made another round. Esther was the one person who always stood beside me no matter what I had done or how much I hurt her. She was the rock I clung to when the waters got rough. But despite all this, I treated her like crap. All those years, she put everything she had into making our marriage work, doing everything in her power to try and help her mixed-up husband, and I was ruining it all. She had such high hopes that after I got off the pills things would get better. And they did—for a little bit. But when they started to go downhill, I began to feel like I may be losing her. That made everything that much worse.

I started wondering if Esther would have been a lot better off without me. Eventually, I convinced myself that she definitely would have been—and would be.

I finally went to a doctor—something I've always been skeptical about because they sometimes seem to be just after my money. But with this doctor, I felt different. I trusted her. She asked me a lot of hard questions. I admitted that I used to get very angry but that lately, I couldn't even muster the energy to do that. I told her I didn't care about anything anymore. I ended up pleading with her for some painkillers, and I will always remember her answer. She said that as a doctor, she couldn't see me if I kept asking for pills—and also that she didn't want to stop seeing me, because that would mean I would go to another doctor. And that other doctor just might give me what I wanted. I felt like she was just being stubborn. It didn't seem fair that she could give me what I told myself would make it all better, but she just wouldn't listen. Almost subconsciously, though, I realized that her not giving me the pills showed she actually cared for me and wanted me to get better. I respected her for that.

Instead of painkillers, she got an appointment with a psychiatrist, who put me on Zoloft and suggested I start counseling. This combination seemed to help slightly, for a while—just enough for Esther to get her hopes up again.

In the end, though, counseling helps, but it doesn't "fix" you. The only person who can change you is *you*. Nobody else. They can help you for a little bit or give you the tools to help, but you are the one who has to do the labor. Counseling can help you a great deal, if you really want it to. It won't be easy. You will have to dig through memories and feelings that you never want to look at again. It will make you sick to your stomach. But if you truly want to get better, you will have to go to the root of the problem. And for me, that was a nasty, rotten root.

It would have saved me and Esther a lot of heartaches if I'd approached counseling in this way at first, but I didn't. I had my mind set that they would make it all better. That I would unload on them, and they would take care of the rest. It didn't work that way. And, because I've always been stubborn, I wanted to do a lot of the personal work alone. This stems from my issues and the fear of not being accepted if people knew my terrible secrets. These secrets were causing a lot of self-loathing, and I was losing all self-respect—a very dangerous and extremely slippery slope to be on. I was in a dark place, and there didn't seem to be any end in sight.

THE LOWEST LOW

One night, Esther had had enough. I have no idea what started it, but one night, I went off in anger again. Poor Esther had finally had enough. She had been through so much pain and suffering, with all her hopes and dreams finally, completely, broken to pieces. We had a furious argument, and I completely lost it. I wasn't so much angry as I was a combination of depressed, frustrated, and unbelievably tired of feeling hopeless. It wasn't that I necessarily wanted to end my life, but I was so sick and tired of suffering that I was absolutely desperate to not feel anymore. I couldn't see any end in sight, and I couldn't begin to imagine what it would be like if I had to live until I was eighty.

I had already made up my mind that I would overdose on heroin. That was my way to end the pain.

I knew Esther would try to change my mind, though. Plus, I didn't have any heroin. Instead, I went for a gun. Something stopped me, though: I didn't want to use a gun, and I wanted one last heroin high. So I sat there, thinking about how to get it. In the meantime, my poor heartbroken wife ran for help. I didn't even realize it at the time. I had lost my grasp on reality, with the only thing in mind being to end the pain. By divine intervention, as Esther was running out of our driveway, my brothers Wes and Paul were just turning in. When they heard what was going on, Wes immediately ran to the house and came straight to my office. Looking back at it now, it always amazes me to think that he hadn't seemed scared or afraid at all. In fact, he was furious. Esther and Wes have always been close friends, and to see her in this way really got to him. He was pretty harsh and told me quite frankly what he thought about my behavior. He told me what a beautiful, loving wife I had and to take a long look at what I was doing to her. He was harsh enough that it slowly brought me back to reality. I did talk to him a little bit about how I felt that Esther would be better off without me, and there was just no use in continuing. He told me this was not my decision to make. Esther had made the decision to marry me, and I was being very unfair to her.

The next day, Esther and I had a long talk, and I felt better after having blown off some steam. She made me promise to get help, and though I didn't think we could afford it, I said that I would. That evening, some more people showed up to talk to me, and the more I was able to talk, the better I felt. I told them that I had promised Esther I would get help. They wanted me to go right away, but I knew that I would have to look for a place that dealt with Amish people and that I would likely have to wait for an opening to get in. I resisted their pleas for me to go to the hospital.

The next afternoon, Esther told me that she was going over to her parents' for a while. After she left, I thought about going for a walk in the woods for a while. That was my usual cure when I was down, just to be in nature and away from everything else. I was still thinking about it when I heard somebody pull into the driveway. I had no idea at the time, but the law had gotten involved and had asked Esther questions: Did she think I would really kill myself? Was it a desperate plea for help? Had I been selling things that were special or sentimental to me?

When she admitted that I had, indeed, been selling import-ant things, the officer told her he needed to get me to the hospital as quickly as possible. When they pulled into the driveway, I knew none of this and assumed they wanted to check up on me. When they told me they were taking me to the hospital, I didn't agree right away. I told them that I needed to talk to Esther first and let her know what was going on. They told me that they had already talked to her about it, and she was fine with it. I didn't want to go, but they told me that it was just for an evaluation and said I might not have to do anything besides some blood work. I finally agreed.

While at the hospital, they took good care of me, asked me some questions, and left me to myself in a small room. They gave me food, drinks, and sleeping pills, but other than that I was isolated. I had to stay at the hospital for seventy-two hours while they decided what they wanted to do with me. I had thought that once I was checked out, they would release me from the hospital and let me go home again. I was pretty worried about missing work and wanted to know where Esther was. Every time I had visitors, I would ask about Esther. At first, they told me that she was getting help, and that she was fine. As time went on, I became more persistent in wanting to talk to her, and I kept being denied. This made me suspicious. I started getting desperate, and all kinds of bad scenarios started running through my head. I thought that Esther had finally had enough of my crap and didn't want anything to do with me anymore. This thought was absolutely crushing, and I didn't want to believe it. But I couldn't think of another reason why she wouldn't call me, and nobody was telling me anything.

It was at the same time that I found out that I would not be going home, but would have to go someplace else first. I didn't know it at the time, but everyone was scrambling around trying to get me into a place that specialized in people from Amish communities, but there simply were no openings available.

When the hospital transported me, I had no idea where I was going or what kind of place it would be. All I knew was that it was a long ride that lasted at least a couple of hours. When I got off the ambulance and they wheeled me inside, I had no idea where I was. If I had known what I was getting into, I would have fought back with every single ounce of energy I had. They would have had to kill or drug me to get me in there. It was a place straight out of a horror movie.

That first night, after I was in bed, a nurse named Oakley came in to check on me. We started talking like two old friends. It felt nice to simply talk to someone again. She gained a lot of my trust that first night—trust that would eventually save my life.

"THIS IS HOW IT FEELS TO LOSE YOUR MIND"
Before entering the mental facility, I had been on 60 mil-

ligrams of Zoloft. Immediately, they switched me directly to 800 milligrams of Seroquel. This certainly didn't help matters at all. This sudden change was dramatic, and the place itself was traumatic. To top it all off, I didn't have anyone to talk to about what I was going through. I would have given anything in the world just to hear Esther's voice again. Every time I asked my visitors about her, they just kind of brushed the questions aside and wouldn't give me a clear answer.

I really couldn't concentrate on my own recovery without knowing where my little lady was and why she didn't want to talk to me. At that point in time, I thought that the only reason that she wouldn't call or visit was because she was done with me. I tried to tell myself that it wasn't true, but I knew that if she truly wanted to talk to me, she would find a way.

The conditions in the facility were nightmarish. At night, there were screams and fighting and cursing. We weren't allowed to close the doors to our rooms, so every time someone walked past, you could see their shadows. It was creepy if they stopped at your door and just stood there. All you could see was their shadow. I would tell myself that it was just a nurse checking on me, but all too often I would hear the words, "Hey, why are you out of your room?" Then the shadow would move away.

One day, something happened that almost made me go

completely insane. I was doing pushups by my bed when, all at once, I saw bare feet right beside me. I always thought that it was a myth that you can feel the hair on the back of your neck stand up, but I am a true believer now. Some kind of instinct warned me before I even looked up. There she was: a naked woman standing in my room, in her eyes an unspeakable evil. The very first thing that went through my mind was that she was going to eat me alive. I seriously thought she was going to eat me, her eyes looking like a cross between a lion and a snake. I have never come close to being as scared as I was in that moment.

Trying not to move too fast, I slowly stood up and we just looked at each other for what seemed like forever. Finally, I reached out very slowly and took her by the elbow. She never moved a single muscle. I led her back to her room and sat her on the bed, then ran back to my own room. I sat on the floor in a corner of my room where I could see the doorway and feel the walls at my back, in shock. I sat there for at least two hours, shaking uncontrollably. Her eyes have never left me. I have nightmares about them to this day.

While in the facility, I had a roommate who claimed that he could see the demons that sat on his shoulders. He hated them because they made him do stuff that he didn't want to do. He would talk with them at all hours of the day and night, sometimes having serious arguments with them. He always wore sunglasses so they couldn't see his eyes, and when the nurses would take them off to check his pupils, he would fight like crazy to keep them. One morning, I woke up to hear him making some weird noises. He sat on the edge of the bed making all kinds of motions. Then, he would point right at my head, make some kind of hissing sound, and crook his finger at me as if he wanted me to follow him. I felt like someone had thrown cold water on me, creeping me out more than I can explain.

The whole time I was there, I cannot recall one second when I felt safe. When I had first gotten there, I asked Oakley how long I would have to stay. She told me it would be until the doctors felt I was stable enough to be released and advised me that no matter what happened, I should try to pretend everything was fine. That way, I could get out sooner. I tried to follow her advice, but it was so hard. The only thing that kept me going was the faint hope that Esther might still call someday. I felt that if I could only hear her voice, it would help tremendously. I was worried sick about her, and nobody would tell me anything. I had to pretend that everything was fine, when on the inside I was screaming for help. Little by little, I was slowly losing my grip on reality. All I ever saw were walls and halls. There was nothing to distinguish on day from the next. The hours and days started to bleed into each other until I couldn't tell the difference. I had nothing to tell me how long I had been there or how long I would still be there. I started to think that I had Alzheimer's or something and nobody was telling me, or that I just didn't remember it if they did tell me. With everything that I saw on a daily basis, all the alarms going off at night, not getting sleep, being scared all the time, and being worried sick about Esther, my brain was getting very close to the breaking point.

I started questioning Oakley about whether I would be there the rest of my life or not. She tried to assure me that I would get to go home someday, that I didn't have Alzheimer's, and that I wasn't losing my mind. I wanted to believe her, but at the same time I knew that if I *was* actually losing my mind and had to stay there the rest of my life, her answer would be the same. One day, I smiled to myself in the mirror and told myself that this was how it felt to lose your mind.

I was so lost and mixed up that I simply made myself accept the fact that I was now alone in this world. About the time that I finally gave in to the fact that Esther didn't want me anymore, something strange happened. Oakley had just come in for her shift, and I asked her for some clothes so I could change when I showered. As she handed me my clothes, I got a very faint whiff of cigarette smoke. She noticed right away that something was different, and when I asked if she had been smoking, she admitted that she had been. She let me smell her hair again so that I could smell it better. I know that it sounds crazy and creepy, but you have no idea how that made me feel. This was the only thing that was different or out of place. It told me that this was *a different day*. Up to that point, there was simply no way to tell the difference. I was absolutely elated! Maybe I wasn't going crazy after all! I didn't want to hope too much, but I just couldn't help myself. When I told Oakley about it, she smiled and just bluntly said, "I told you so!"

The next day when she came in for her shift, she brought in an energy drink for me, saying, "Look, different day!" It's crazy that such a tiny little thing can change your outlook on life. All it took was a very faint smell of cigarette smoke, that whiff of proof. Now that I felt that maybe someday I could leave, I began wondering if Esther would take me back. I had been led to believe that the doctors didn't want Esther to call or visit because they were afraid that it would destabilize me again. This didn't really make sense to me, but I had nobody to ask whether this was really true or not.

One day, I had enough. I was in very bad mood. Alarms had been going off all night, and I was sick and tired of being scared and helpless. I'm not sure what started it, but a nurse said something that infuriated me. I grabbed her around the shoulders and pinned her against the wall. I was screaming at her, letting out all the frustration. I yelled something about them keeping me until I was better, but there was no way that I could get better without knowing what was going on with Esther. And since they wouldn't let her call or visit, I was going to stay there forever anyway. As soon as that came out, I saw instantly that I had said something out of place. The nurse that I pinned just blinked and gave a quick sideways glance at another nurse standing to my right. I'm pretty good at reading faces and eyes, and I knew something wasn't quite right. I let go of the nurse I was holding and stepped back. I looked at them both and told them that I knew that I had said something weird and I wanted to know what it was.

Oakley and another nurse took me to a couch and wanted to know who had told me that Esther couldn't call or visit. In that instant I saw the awful truth. Before they even started to explain, I already knew. They told me that they had absolutely no legal right to tell me who could call or visit. That was my decision, and mine alone. Nobody else could do that. I said, "So either somebody isn't telling me the truth, or Esther doesn't want to see me." Neither one of them answered me, though we all knew that those were the only options. Oakley later told me that as much as I talked about Esther and how much she meant to me, that she always thought it odd that she never called or came to visit. They both told me that if I felt it would help my recovery, I should do whatever I could to see her or talk to her.

"But what if it's her that doesn't want to see me and everyone is just covering for her?" I asked Oakley. She gave me a hug and told me that if that was what was going on, I would have to accept it and try to move on. This thought was almost more than I could take. I ran back to my room and sat in my trusty little corner, crying with bitterness at the unfairness of it all. I knew that I had been misled, and now I didn't know who to trust or where to turn. I was so lonely that I seriously thought about ending it all.

The next day, I had visitors and again pleaded to see Esther. They told me they'd bring her along the next day. I was so relieved to hear this that it was all I could think about. I was jittery and nervous and didn't get much sleep that night, trying to remember what she smelled like. I was also extremely worried about her reaction. I still had a bad feeling about her not wanting to see me, and though I tried hard not to dwell on that, it was always at the back of my mind.

The next morning, I was in the common room long before anybody else was even awake. The nurses got a kick out of how excited I was. They kept telling me to calm down, that Esther would be here soon enough. Throughout the morning, they kept joking with me about it. As visiting hours drew closer, the more nervous I got. By the time they rolled around, I was almost a wreck. Finally, the hour arrived when they were supposed to be there. After the first ten minutes, I started getting nervous about them not showing up. The nurses kept telling me to calm down, that they probably got stuck in traffic or something.

As more and more time went by, they started running out of excuses. They started getting quiet and not saying much and always seemed to be busy when I was around. I did notice that as time drew on that they never really left me alone by myself, and that there was always one of them in the vicinity. This made it even worse because it told me that they didn't think she was coming anymore and they were keeping a close watch on me in case I did something stupid. Finally, visiting hours were over, and nobody had showed up.

I had always known that there were only two reasons that Esther wouldn't call or visit: either somebody was telling her that she couldn't or she simply didn't want to. Because I had been told that she could visit and she hadn't, that left only one option. Obviously, I automatically assumed she didn't want to. I was absolutely, totally, completely crushed. I went back to my room and lay on my bed and cried my heart out. Because I was so depressed, the nurses had to keep watch over me at all times. They took one-hour shifts on a chair beside my bed. I cried for a little over four hours straight, and every one of the nurses cried with me as they watched over me. The thought that Esther didn't want me anymore was more than I could take. I knew that I was only making things worse for myself by crying and seeming to be unstable, but I couldn't take it anymore. I was completely heartbroken, and just couldn't stop crying. I felt so lonely and hopeless that there just didn't seem to be any point in trying anymore. All the frustration, the helplessness, the horror, the loneliness, and the feeling of total rejection boiled to the surface.

The next morning, I made up my mind. I told the nurses

that I wouldn't accept any visitors or phone calls unless it was Esther. That evening, I kept leaving messages at home, begging and pleading for Esther to call me. By some kind of miracle, she happened to be at home by herself, and after about the twentieth try, she happened to hear the phone and picked up! I couldn't even talk at first! I just wanted to sit and listen to her voice. That was a very confusing and emotional phone call. I wanted to know why she didn't love me anymore, and she had no idea what I was talking about. At first, I assumed she was skating around the truth, because she obviously never called or came to visit, but little by little our stories came out. She told me that the person advising the friends and family had told them not to let her have any connection with me while I was in the facility.

We found out later that somehow wires had gotten crossed, and the advisor had never said anything like that. It had all been a misunderstanding. In fact, the next day Esther and our family went to talk with the advisor. When he realized that she had never been to see me, he was astonished. He told the family to get her down to see me as soon as possible. While they were having their conference with him, I was busy with my own plans. A nurse had given me a very important piece of information that morning. I don't think that she was supposed to tell me about it, but she told me that I could probably leave AMA (against medical advice). When I told the head nurse that I wanted the paperwork so that I could leave AMA, she called in the psychiatrist, who immediately wanted to know where I had heard of that. I didn't answer her. I just asked her if she was going to deny me or not. She didn't like it at all, but there was nothing that she could do.

She handed me the paperwork, and I had it filled out in a hurry. They told me that it would take a couple hours before they would get back to me; that was the most stressful wait that I have ever had. While I was waiting, I called Bennie and told him that there was a chance that I might be released. He told me to let him know and he would immediately come and pick me up. After what seemed like forever (but was actually only a couple of hours), they brought back my paperwork and told me that I could leave as soon as I had filled out some more paperwork. It didn't sink in for a while that I was actually leaving! I really thought that at the last minute something would come up and I would have to stay there. I had suffered so many setbacks and heartaches that I truly didn't think that I would make it out alive.

When Bennie showed up to take me home, he saw how tightly strung I was. He told me later that as we were coming down the elevator, he could tell that I was ready to run at the slightest sign that they might still keep me. I was so keyed up that I can guarantee you that if a nurse had said as much as a loud "hey," I would have taken off. There was no way they were getting me back in there.

When we finally walked outside, it had rained a little bit, and I will never forget the smell of wet asphalt mixed with wet rubber and a slight smell of what might have been spilled pop. It was the best fragrance I have ever smelled in my life. I still think about that every time I smell wet asphalt.

Esther was at Bennie's, and it wasn't until I saw her that I started to believe that I was actually out and wouldn't have to go back. It all just seemed like a dream. Esther told me later that it almost broke her heart to see how cold and emotionless I was. She said it seemed like I was completely empty and void of any feeling whatsoever. I can believe it. While I was in the facility, I had to harden myself against everything that I saw and felt just to survive. My mind wouldn't have taken it if I hadn't. It was a defense mechanism, but I had done it long enough that it became a part of me. I couldn't trust enough to let my emotions through.

It took a while before I even trusted Esther. I was broken enough that it took a while before we could even start putting my pieces back together again, but with my strong little lady by my side to help me every step of the way, we made it.

NOT OUT OF THE WOODS YET

Both good and bad came from that experience. Even though I know the place has long since been shut down, I'm still afraid of it. On the other hand, it brought me and Esther closer together. I will never again take her love for granted. I will never forget how it felt to think that I was losing her. It makes the time we spend together that much more special. It also gave me a perspective on how important it is for the Amish and Mennonites to have places that take our religion and culture into perspective when dealing with us. Just the cultural shock was bad enough when I was there, let alone all the other pieces. Just thinking about taking an Amish teenage girl or boy, and leaving them there, makes my skin crawl.

My first week out of the facility, I didn't like to let Esther get out of my sight. If I didn't see her for too long, I started getting uptight and nervous. After I got out, we were advised to go take counseling together. It was obvious that I needed serious help, and by this time, I was willing to try anything as long as Esther went with me. Family and friends recommended a place in North Carolina called Door of Hope. Esther got a reservation for a weeklong stay there. That was a hard week for me because I had to look deep inside and see all the pus and poison that I had stored up.

Our counselor was a man named Joe, and I simply couldn't open up to a man. I wanted to blame it on everything except what had happened when I was young. I blamed it on the drugs, even though I'd had serious depression and trust issues a long time before I even started taking pills. It's sad but once again, I simply blocked somebody from helping because it was more painful to look at what had happened than it was to just keep living with my horrible trash. I was just too stubborn and had been living with it for so long that it became a part of who I was. I'm ashamed to admit that I didn't get much help down there simply because I wouldn't open up about the abuse.

Even though I wasn't quite ready to let go, they were able to help Esther tremendously. She put all her effort into therapy and was able to find peace. This became very obvious once we were back home. Before, when I had gotten frustrated or lost my tempter, she would get tired of it and snap back. After that week, she was a different person. Absolutely nothing could shake her faith in God and what He had done for her. If I hurt her or snapped at her, she would simply turn away; I would see her lips moving and know that she was praying for me. That sight hurt me because I often felt like I didn't deserve her love. At the same time, I saw the inner peace that she had. I wanted that same peace so badly, but I just didn't know how to get it.

A TURNING POINT

I have often wondered why it is so hard to let go of past trauma. Is it because we are afraid of what people will say? Is it because we are ashamed? For me, it had a lot to do with the fact that mine happened when I was so young. As a kid, I didn't know how badly it was affecting me. By the time I started realizing that I had serious problems, I had already gotten so used to blocking that part off that I didn't even recognize what I was doing. Even when I was depressed, I could usually put up a pretty good front when I was around family or friends. Esther once asked me how I could have two personalities, and the answer is simple: I have a lifetime experience in acting.

Eventually, that changed. Gradually, little by little, Esther helped me take baby steps in the right direction. I had always been a "why me" person. I felt that God had given me a rough path to walk on, and I would wonder why some people had it all while I had to struggle. We had no kids and no money. Where was the fairness in that? Slowly, I came to see that we all get dealt different hands in life, and how we deal with our problems is our own choice.

As my beautiful wife slowly kept chipping away at my scars, she started seeing what was underneath—and she was horrified. I think sometimes it hurt her more than it hurt me, but it brought us so much closer together to be able to heal together.

One day, out of the blue, she asked me why I didn't like men. It was unexpected enough that I hesitated, and she knew to keep pressing. I told her about the hairy arms and how they still triggered me from time to time. We spent a long time talking about what happened, and I slowly released a lot of those pent-up feelings I had been trying to block out for most of my life. It was the strangest release of emotions I have ever felt. Even though it was Esther I was talking to, it still felt strange to actually be talking to someone about the abuse. I think it was the combination of fully trusting someone and dealing with overwhelming shame. That first time was so hard, but she kept me talking about it—never pushing hard, but taking my hand and leading me through piece by piece. Talking about it was the first huge step toward recovery, but I still had a long way to go before I could actually let go.

Just having Esther helping to share my heavy load and to share the pain with me made a such a big difference that I can't put it into words. There were times I didn't want to talk about something because I thought that it would only bring her down, but it didn't work that way at all. Esther is such a strong person. She is exactly who I need as I walk this twisted path. With God above me and her beside me, I don't need anything else.

CHAPTER EIGHT

Stepping into the Light

Finally Finding My Way Home

One evening, I almost lost it again to depression. Absolutely nothing was going the way I had envisioned. One problem after another kept piling up until I didn't know which way to turn.

Esther was already at work that morning, and I'd just awoken from a fitful sleep. I got tears in my eyes as soon as I realized that I would have to get up and face the world—that's how depressed I was that I had even woken up. By the time I was dressed, the tears had turned into a full-blown cry. I just simply couldn't go on. It wasn't possible.

I finally got on my knees and poured it all out to Him. I didn't hold anything back. I got mad and frustrated, but I let it all out and laid it at His feet. I had finally hit the bottom, and this stubborn, headstrong kid finally had to give up and let Him take over. That was exactly where He wanted me! As long as I tried to do it all by myself, I wasn't letting Him help. I told myself that I trusted Him, but I never gave up the reins. I wanted to drive and let Him tell me where to go. It doesn't work that way. You have to let Him drive and trust that He knows where He is going. I was so stubborn that He had to break me down little by little until I finally, wholly, broke. Only then could He build me back up into what He wanted me to be.

After I was done with my prayer, I was so broken that I couldn't even stand up, so I just knelt there, crying. Suddenly, a calm feeling came over me. I am very ashamed to admit that the first thing I thought of was if I had accidentally taken a Perk 30. I knew it wasn't possible, but that's how strong the feeling was. It finally sank in that He was right there with me. The feeling was so good that I actually laughed. It was absolutely amazing. I felt at ease in letting Him take over and handle all the responsibilities.

In Ephesians 4:23–24, it says, "And be renewed in the spirit of your mind. And that ye put on the new man, which after God is created in righteousness and true holiness." I didn't even realize it then, but that's what I was doing. I was putting on the new man and completely changing my outlook on life. In putting all my trust in Him, it totally changed how I approached my everyday problems. If something didn't go how I expected it to, it didn't faze me at all. I know that He knows exactly what He is doing. I don't have to understand or question why. I know that He always has my best interests at heart. It makes it so much easier if He carries all the stress and takes the whole load. All I have to do is follow. All those wasted years could have been a whole lot different if I had only trusted. I can't look at it like that, though. What happened, happened. It is all in the past. I can't change that, but I can learn from it, and put that to use in helping others who might be going through what I went through.

It's not our mistakes that define who we are. It is what we learn from them.

INTO THE HERE AND NOW

After fully accepting God, my life just kept getting better. I felt so good that I started cutting back on my bipolar meds. I gradually kept cutting back until I was only taking a tiny amount in the evening before I went to bed. After that, I reached out to my psychiatrist and asked to be on something less strong. He obliged—and I barely took it. I stopped altogether.

After I had been med-free for a while, I asked Esther one

evening how she thought that I was doing on the new pills. After I let her gush for a little bit about how good I was doing, I told her I hadn't been taking any for a while. At first she didn't believe me, but when she saw I was serious, she had mixed emotions: I knew she was happy for me, but also afraid of what may happen.

This was one time those fears, though justified, would be unfounded.

Something happened soon after that—something that proved to her I was really better. My foreman, Levi, put in his two-week notice. It made my job seem almost impossible, but I had to respect his choice. If it was something that he didn't really want to do, then I was glad that he was strong enough to make the decision to quit. Too many times we don't like what we're doing but keep doing it because we think we should, or simply because the money is good. Though I was losing an unbelievable worker and crew leader, I was glad that he was making his own way in this world.

That night, I sat down and had a talk with Esther. I told her that with Levi quitting, I wouldn't be able to help much around the house anymore. I explained to her that from now on I would have to do all my estimates on Saturdays and do all my paperwork in the evenings after work. We had a long talk, and she later told me that she was amazed how calm and upbeat I was. She commented that if that had happened a couple of months earlier, I would have been depressed and ready to just quit everything. It proved to us both just how much my attitude had changed. I completely trusted God and knew that He knew what He was doing, even if it didn't make sense to me yet.

And, as always, my little lady completely supported me and promised to shoulder even more than what she was already doing. She is the manager at the Swiss Maid fry pie factory and always has a lot on her mind, getting all the orders ready and making sure that everything is running smoothly on the floor. She usually gets up between one o'clock and three o'clock in the morning and is long gone by the time I get up. What time she gets home all depends on how many pies they have to make that day. Their record is a little over eight thousand fry pies in a day. That was a long day—but she loves her job, and I'm proud of her.

With Esther working in the mornings and me gone on Saturdays, sometimes it feels like we are ships passing in the night, but it makes the time we do spend together just that much more precious.

OUR FUTURE

With me being on drugs all the time and battling depression, our thoughts of having children had been, understandably, put on the backburner for those years.

After I was well, we approached the topic again. We both knew we wanted children—but it simply wasn't happening. I was nervous to go to the doctor because I was worried the problem may be on my end, and I didn't want to do that to Esther. But finally, we went in to get the tests done.

Esther made sure to tell the doctor that I had been made fun of in the past for not being "man enough" to have kids. The doctor made it very clear to me that no matter how the results came back, I should never blame myself for the results or listen to what other people said about me.

We had to wait a week for the results. As soon as we walked into her office, I could see right away the answer was one I didn't want to hear. Her face was happy to see us, but her eyes were sad. Although I had already suspected the news, to hear it was quite a shock. Esther cried a little bit, too, and we hugged.

We asked the doctor why, and she said she didn't know—but the odds were pretty much zero. She told me that it was just one of those medical mysteries, and I just needed to trust in God and if He wanted me to have children, then He would give me some.

The only thing I could think about on the way home was that I would never hold my own little daughter. Never help her tie her shoes, never take her kayaking, never teach her how to swim. I was able to hold it together till I got home, but it was a struggle. Once I was by myself, I lost it. Knowing that my little lady had the same hopes and dreams as I did just made it that much harder to accept.

Eventually, I gathered together the pieces of my heart and went to face the world. Once we knew for sure we couldn't have children, we didn't keep getting our hopes up anymore. The only time that it was really hard for me was when my brother and his wife had their first child. I had secretly been hoping it wouldn't be a baby girl because I knew how much that would hurt. I knew I was being selfish, but I couldn't help it. Of course, they had the most beautiful little girl. I didn't want to go over that first night simply because I was afraid that I would start crying again.

I almost did. When I held that precious little bundle in my hands and felt her warmth, it almost started again. The only thing that kept me from crying was how happy I was for Owen and Susan. Their happiness was very contagious and made me feel like a part of it all. Little Maria has been such an unbelievable bright spot in my life. I love that little blonde-haired girl like my very own. I tease her every chance I get, and will never tire of reading her favorite book to her, which is *The Jungle Book*. I love to spoil her, and for some reason whenever she comes over, she says she's hungry. I know that she has me wrapped around her finger, but I don't care.

Today, instead of dwelling on the pain and what I don't have, I try instead to concentrate on what I *do* have. Not that I wouldn't take a little girl. I would take one in a heartbeat, but it is easier if I look at what a close relationship me and my little lady have. All that we have been through has forged our love into something very precious.

To me, love is lying on a hot sandbar in the river, watching my little lady try to catch the minnows around her feet. Love is teaching her to drive excavating equipment and watching her get it stuck. Love is locking her out of the house and then making her dance before letting her back in. Love is getting a severe tongue lashing for making her dance before letting her in. Love is letting her doze off, then waking her up and asking her if she's asleep. I love everything we do together. I'm simply not complete when she's not around. It always feels like something's missing.

I made it through all the struggles in my life to get here to this place, with God and my Esther. The path has not been a straight one, but the destination is beautiful.

Conclusion

Even if you haven't gone through addiction or abuse, we all have challenges. My ask, again, is that we all treat each other with a little more grace. You never know what someone has been through.

If you *have* gone through even a piece of what I went through, please don't give up hope. Don't be afraid to ask for help. If you can't turn to God like I did, turn to whatever you believe in that gives you hope and comfort. If you're thinking about toying with drugs, just don't. I'm not trying to preach to you. I know I'm not a perfect man, and that is an understatement. I have seen things and done things that are beyond awful. But if sharing those things and my story helps even one person, it is worth it.

Today, I am clean, I'm with my lovely wife, and things are

great. I'm living a life I used to only imagine. We don't have much money or worldly possessions, but we have each other, and that's worth more than anything I could ever ask for. I wouldn't trade it for anything in the world. I still have my struggles, especially in the winter, so keep me in your prayers. I will keep you in mine.

Acknowledgments

First and foremost, I want to thank God for guiding me through this life and keeping me safe throughout. A very special thanks to my beautiful, patient, loving little lady. Esther, you literally saved my life more than once. Thank you for that, and also for keeping the coffee pot filled while I was writing this book. Thank you to all our family and friends for all the things that you have helped us through. Thanks to my mom and dad, who put up with a very rebellious kid. A special thanks to Marsha Lyons for pushing me when I felt like giving up. A heartfelt thank you to Ron and Charlotte Birchel for helping us through our great time of need. You will never know how much you truly helped. Thank you to everyone—known and unknown—who donated enough money to put me through rehab. Without you, this book would never have gotten written. Thank you to Greg, Laura, Reggie, and everyone at work for keeping an eye on me and helping to keep me on an even keel today.

Thank you to everyone from the Scribe Media family, especially Maggie, who was always there to answer any one of my hundreds of questions and guide me through a totally foreign landscape. From the bottom of my heart I want to say thank you to Jessica Burdg, who helped me turn this very rough manuscript into a book, calmed my nerves, and supported me when I felt lost. You went way above and beyond the call of duty to help me stay focused on the reason I was writing this book, especially when I wanted to chicken out or was doubting myself. All I can say is thank you. The perfect example of who Jessica is as a person is her own book, *More Than a Diagnosis*. I would highly recommend reading this book, especially for anyone with children who have special needs.

All I can say is thank you, everyone, for your support, through rehab, until now, and moving forward. Thank you.

Made in the USA
Middletown, DE
03 May 2021